*Our thanks to the following reviewers
for their perceptive comments:*

James Cagnacci
City College of San Francisco

Thomas Carnicelli
University of New Hampshire

Marcia Curtis
University of Massachusetts–Amherst

Ernest Johansson
Ohio University

Michael Meyer
University of Connecticut

Allan Ramsay
Central Missouri State University

Monroe Roth
Lehigh County Community College,
Pennsylvania

Jocelyn Siler
University of Montana

Bennett Yohe
Red Rocks Community College,
Colorado

Bernice Zelditch
Foothill College,
California

A
WRITER'S
REFERENCE

Diana Hacker

A BEDFORD BOOK

ST. MARTIN'S PRESS • NEW YORK

FOR BEDFORD BOOKS

Publisher: Charles H. Christensen
Associate Publisher: Joan E. Feinberg
Managing Editor: Elizabeth M. Schaaf
Copyeditor: Barbara G. Flanagan
Text design: Claire Seng-Niemoeller
Cover design: Richard Emery

Library of Congress Catalog Card Number: 88-70947

3   2   1   0
f   e

For information write: St. Martin's Press, Inc.
175 Fifth Avenue, New York, NY 10010

Editorial Offices: Bedford Books of St. Martin's Press
29 Winchester Street, Boston, MA 02116

ISBN: 0-312-02455-X

ACKNOWLEDGMENTS
The American Heritage Dictionary of the English Language, from the entry under "prevent." Copyright © 1978 by Houghton Mifflin Company. Reprinted by permission.
Russell Baker, from "Poor Russell's Almanac," copyright © 1972 by The New York Times Company. Reprinted by permission.
Jane Brody, from *Jane Brody's Nutrition Book.* Copyright © 1981 by Jane E. Brody. Reprinted by permission of W. W. Norton & Company, Inc.
Roger Caras, from "What's a Koala?" Copyright 1983 by Roger Caras. First appeared in *Geo* Magazine, May 1983. Reprinted by permission of Roberta Pryor, Inc.
Bruce Catton, from "Grant and Lee: A Study in Contrasts," *The American Story,* Earl Schenck Miers, editor, © 1956 by Broadcast Music, Inc. Reprinted by permission of the U.S. Capitol Historical Society.
Barnaby Conrad III, from " 'Train of Kings, the King of Trains' Is Back on Track," *Smithsonian,* December 1983. Reprinted by permission of *Smithsonian.*
Earl Conrad, from *Harriet Tubman.* Reprinted by permission of Paul S. Erikson, Publisher.
Erik Eckholm, from "Pygmy Chimp Readily Learns Language Skill," *The New York Times.* Copyright © 1985 by The New York Times Company. Reprinted by permission.

Acknowledgments and copyrights are continued on page 208, which constitutes an extension of the copyright page.

Contents

G

M

D

C

Composing
and Revising

C

Composing and Revising

Since it's not possible to think about everything all at once, most experienced writers handle a piece of writing in stages. Roughly speaking, those stages are planning, drafting, and revising.

C1

Planning

C1-a Assess the writing situation.

Begin by taking a look at the writing situation in which you find yourself. The following checklist will help you get started.

Subject

1. How broadly must you cover the subject? Might you narrow it to a more specific topic?
2. How detailed should your coverage be?
3. Where will your information come from? From personal experience? Direct observation? Interviews? Questionnaires? Reading?

Purpose

4. Why are you writing? Do you hope to inform readers, to persuade them, to entertain them, to call them to action — or some combination of these?

Audience

5. Who are your readers?
6. How much do they already know about your subject?
7. How interested and attentive are they likely to be?
8. Will they resist any of your ideas?
9. How close a relationship with them can you assume?
10. How sophisticated are they as readers? Do they have large vocabularies? Can they process long and complex sentences?

Length and format

11. Are you working within any length specifications? If not, what length seems appropriate, given your subject, your purpose, and your audience?

12. Must you use a particular format? Some possible formats in the academic world are essays, lab reports, case studies, and research papers. Some possible formats in the business world are letters, résumés, memos, reports, and proposals.
13. Will your subject be more accessible to readers if you use visual devices such as headings, lists, charts, graphs, and diagrams?

C1-b Experiment with techniques for exploring ideas.

Instead of just plunging into a first draft, experiment with one or more techniques for exploring your subject — perhaps listing, clustering, branching, or asking questions. Whatever technique you turn to, the goal is the same: to generate a wealth of ideas. At this early stage of the writing process, you should aim for quantity, not necessarily quality, of ideas. If an idea proves to be off the point, trivial, or too farfetched, you can always throw it out later.

Listing

You might begin by simply listing ideas, putting them down in the order in which they occur to you — a technique sometimes known as "brainstorming." Here, for example, is a list one writer jotted down:

Lifeguarding — an ideal summer job?

> my love of swimming and lying in the sun
>
> hired by Powdermill Village, an apartment complex
>
> first, though, there was a test
>
> two weeks of training — grueling physical punishment plus book work
>
> I passed. The work was over — or so I thought.
>
> greeted by manager; handed a broom, hose, bottle of disinfectant
>
> scrubbing bathrooms, cleaning the pool, clearing the deck of dirt and leaves
>
> little kids breaking every pool rule in the book — running on deck, hanging on buoyed ropes, trying to drown each other
>
> spent most of my time blowing the whistle
>
> working the evening shift no better — adults smuggling in gin and tonics, sexual advances from married men
>
> by end of day, a headache and broom-handled hands

The ideas appear here in the order in which they first occurred to the writer. Later she felt free to rearrange them, to cluster them under general categories, to delete some, and to add others. In other words, she treated her initial list as a source of ideas and a springboard to new ideas, not as a formal outline.

Clustering and branching

Unlike listing, the techniques of clustering and branching highlight relationships among ideas. To cluster ideas, write your topic in the center of a sheet of paper, draw a circle around it, and surround that circle with related ideas connected to it with lines. If some of the satellite ideas lead to more specific clusters, write them down as well. The writer of the following diagram was exploring ideas for an essay on home uses for computers.

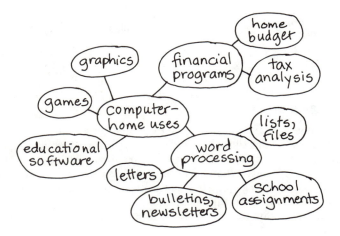

To use the branching technique, put the main idea at the top of a page and then list major supporting ideas beneath it, leaving plenty of space between ideas. To the right of each major idea, branch out to minor ideas, drawing lines to indicate the connections. If minor ideas lead to even more specific ideas, continue branching. Here, for example, is a branching diagram for a newspaper article describing an innovative magnet high school called "School without Walls."

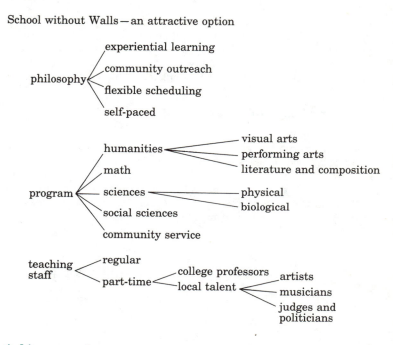

School without Walls — an attractive option

Asking questions

By asking relevant questions, you can generate many ideas — and you can make sure that you have adequately surveyed your subject. When gathering material for a story, journalists routinely ask themselves Who? What? When? Where? Why? and How? In addition to helping journalists get started, these questions ensure that they will not overlook an important fact: the date of a prospective summit meeting, for example, or the exact location of a neighborhood burglary.

Whenever you are writing about events, whether current or historical, the journalist's questions are one way to get started. One student, whose subject was the reaction in 1915 to D. W. Griffith's silent film *The Birth of a Nation,* began exploring her topic with this set of questions:

Who objected to the film?

What were the objections?

When were protests first voiced?

Where were protests most strongly expressed?

Why did protesters object to the film?

How did protesters make their views known?

In the academic world, scholars often generate ideas with specific questions related to their discipline: one set of questions for analyzing short stories, another for evaluating experiments in social psychology, still another for reporting field experiences in anthropology. If you are writing in a particular discipline, try to discover the questions that scholars typically explore. These are frequently presented in textbooks as checklists.

C1-c Settle on a tentative focus.

The focus of a piece of writing is its central idea. For many types of writing, the central idea can be asserted in one sentence, a generalization preparing readers for the supporting details that will follow. Such a sentence, which often appears in the opening paragraph, is called a *thesis*. A successful thesis, like the following — taken from an article in *Smithsonian* — points both the writer and the reader in a definite direction:

> Much maligned and the subject of unwarranted fears, most bats are harmless and highly beneficial.

Frequently a thesis sentence outlines the major sections of a piece of writing, a technique known as *blueprinting*. The following thesis sentence prepares readers for a three-part report on the roles a Vietnamese woman is expected to fulfill as she grows up.

> From the moment her mind is mature enough to understand commands, to the day she is married off, to the time when she bears children, a Vietnamese woman continuously tries to establish a good name as a diligent daughter, a submissive wife, and an altruistic mother.

It is a good idea to formulate a thesis early in the writing process, perhaps by jotting it on scratch paper, by putting it at the head of a rough outline, or by attempting an introductory paragraph. But be prepared to reformulate the thesis, if necessary, as your drafts evolve. Keep in mind that a thesis should be

1. more general than the material supporting it,
2. limited enough to be supported in the space allowed, and
3. an accurate reflection of your main point.

Because a thesis must prepare readers for facts and details, it cannot itself be a fact. It must always be a generalization requiring proof or further development.

TOO FACTUAL   The first polygraph was developed by Dr. John A. Larson in 1921.

REVISED   Because the polygraph has not been proved reliable, even under the most controlled conditions, its use by private employers should be banned.

Although a thesis must be a generalization, it must not be *too* general.

TOO BROAD   Many drugs are now being used successfully to treat mental illnesses.

REVISED   Despite its risks and side effects, lithium is currently the most effective treatment for depression.

For some types of writing, it may be difficult or impossible to express the central idea in a thesis sentence; or it may be unwise or unnecessary to put a thesis sentence in the paper itself. A personal narrative, for example, may have a focus too subtle to be capsulized in a single sentence, and such a sentence might ruin the story. Strictly informative writing, like that found in many business memos, may be difficult to summarize in a thesis. In such instances, do not try to force the central idea into a thesis sentence. Instead, think in terms of an overriding purpose, which may or may not be stated directly in the paper itself.

C1-d Sketch a tentative plan.

After you have generated some ideas and formulated a tentative thesis, you may want to construct an outline. The outline might be informal, consisting of the thesis and its major supporting ideas:

Hawaii is losing its cultural identity.

   pure-blooded Hawaiians increasingly rare
   native language diluted
   natives forced off ancestral lands
   little emphasis on native culture in schools
   customs exaggerated and distorted by tourism

For complex writing tasks, however, a formal outline provides a clearer blueprint. The following formal outline brought order to the complexities of a difficult subject, proposed methods for limiting and disposing of nuclear waste.

Thesis: Although various methods for limiting or disposing of nuclear wastes have been proposed, each has serious drawbacks.

I.   Limiting nuclear waste: partitioning and transmutation
   A.   The process is complex and costly.
   B.   Radiation exposure to nuclear workers would increase.

II.   Antarctic ice sheet disposal
   A.   Our understanding of the behavior of ice sheets is too limited.
   B.   An international treaty prohibits disposal in Antarctica.

III.   Space disposal
   A.   The risk of an accident and resulting worldwide disaster is great.
   B.   The cost is prohibitive.
   C.   The method would be unpopular at home and abroad.

IV.   Seabed disposal
   A.   Scientists have not yet solved technical difficulties.
   B.   We do not fully understand the impact of such disposal on the ocean's ecology.

V.   Deep underground disposal
   A.   There is much political pressure against the plan from citizens who do not want their states to become nuclear dumps.
   B.   Geologists disagree about the safest disposal sites.

In constructing a formal outline, keep the following guidelines in mind:

1. Put the thesis at the top.
2. Use parallel grammatical structure for parallel ideas. (See E1.)
3. Use sentences unless phrases are clear.

4. Use the conventional system of numbers and letters for the levels of generality:

I.
   A.
   B.
      1.
      2.
         a.
         b.
            (1)
            (2)
               (a)
               (b)
II.

5. Always use at least two subdivisions for a category.
6. Limit the number of major sections in the outline; if the list of roman numerals grows too long, find some way of clustering the items into a few major categories with more subcategories.
7. Be flexible. Treat your outline as a tentative plan that may need to be revised once you begin drafting.

C2

Drafting

As you rough out an initial draft, keep your planning materials — lists, diagrams, outlines, and so on — close at hand. In addition to helping you get started, such notes and blueprints will encourage you to keep moving. Writing tends to flow better when it is drafted relatively quickly, without many starts and stops.

For most kinds of writing, an introduction announces the main point, several body paragraphs develop it, and a conclusion drives it home. You can begin drafting, however, at any point.

C2-a Draft an introduction.

Your introduction will usually be a paragraph of 50 to 150 words. Perhaps the most common strategy is to open the paragraph with a few sentences that engage the reader and to conclude it with a statement of your main point. The sentence stating the main point is called a *thesis* (see C1-c). In the following example, the thesis has been italicized.

> To the Australian aborigines, the Dreamtime was the time of creation. It was then that the creatures of the earth, including man, came into being. There are many legends about that mystical period, but unfortunately, the koala does not fare too well in any of them. *Slow-witted though it is in life, the koala is generally depicted in myth and folklore as a trickster and a thief.*
> —Roger Caras, "What's a Koala?"

Ideally, the sentences leading to the thesis should hook the reader, perhaps with one of the following:

a startling statistic or unusual fact

a vivid example

a description

a paradoxical statement

a quotation or bit of dialogue

a question

an analogy

a joke or an anecdote

Such hooks are particularly important when you cannot assume your reader's interest in the subject. Hooks are less necessary in scholarly essays and other writing aimed at readers with a professional interest in the subject.

Although the thesis frequently appears at the end of the introduction, it can just as easily appear at the beginning. Much work-related writing, in which a straightforward approach is most effective, commonly begins with the thesis.

> *Flex-time scheduling, which has proved its effectiveness at the Library of Congress, should be introduced on a trial basis at the main branch of the Montgomery County Public Library.* By offering flexible work hours, the library can boost employee morale, cut down on absenteeism, and expand its hours of operation.
> —David Warren, library employee

In narrative and descriptive writing, it is not always necessary to have an explicitly stated thesis. (See C1-c.) However, an introduction without a thesis should clearly suggest the purpose and direction of the essay to follow.

C2-b Draft the body paragraphs.

Body paragraphs are clusters of information in support of an essay's main point. Aim for paragraphs that are unified, well developed, organized, coherent, and neither too long nor too short for easy reading.

Paragraph unity

A paragraph should be unified around a main point. The point should be clear to readers, and all sentences in the paragraph must relate to it.

As a rule, state the main point of a paragraph in a topic sentence — a one-sentence summary that tells readers what to expect as they read on. Usually the topic sentence comes first:

> *Nearly all living creatures manage some form of communication.* The dance patterns of bees in their hive help to point the way to distant flower fields or announce successful foraging. Male stickleback fish regularly swim upside-down to indicate outrage in a courtship contest. Male deer and lemurs mark territorial ownership by rubbing their own body secretions on boundary stones or trees. Everyone has seen a frightened dog put his tail between his legs and run in panic. We, too, use gestures, expressions, postures, and movement to give our words point.
> — Olivia Vlahos, *Human Beginnings*

Although the topic sentence usually comes first, sometimes it follows a transitional sentence linking the paragraph to earlier material, and occasionally it is withheld until the end of the paragraph. And at times a topic sentence is not needed: if a paragraph continues developing an idea clearly introduced in an earlier paragraph, if the details of the paragraph unmistakably suggest its main point, or if the paragraph appears in a narrative of events where generalizations might interrupt the flow of the story.

Sentences that stray from a paragraph's main point destroy its unity. In the following paragraph describing the inadequate facilities in a high school, the information about the typing instructor (in italics) is clearly off the point.

> As the result of tax cuts, the educational facilities of Lincoln High School have reached an all-time low. Some of the books date

back to 1970 and have long since shed their covers. The lack of lab equipment makes it necessary for four to five students to work at one table, with most watching rather than performing experiments. The few typewriters in working order have not been cleaned in so long that most letters come out blotchy and hard to read. There is only one self-correcting typewriter and no prospect of the school's ordering a word processor or computer anytime soon. *Also, the typing instructor left to have a baby at the beginning of the semester, and most of the students don't like the substitute.* As for the furniture, many of the upright chairs have become recliners, and the desk legs are so unbalanced that they play seesaw on the floor.

Paragraph development

Though an occasional short paragraph is fine, particularly if it functions as a transition or emphasizes a point, a series of brief paragraphs suggests inadequate development. How much development is enough? That varies, depending on the writer's purpose and audience.

For example, when she wrote a paragraph attempting to convince readers that it is impossible to lose fat quickly, health columnist Jane Brody knew that she would have to present a great deal of evidence because many dieters want to believe the opposite. She did *not* write:

> When you think about it, it's impossible to lose — as many diets suggest — 10 pounds of *fat* in ten days, even on a total fast. Even a moderately active person cannot lose so much weight so fast. A less active person hasn't a prayer.

This three-sentence paragraph is too skimpy to be convincing. But the paragraph that Brody in fact wrote contains enough evidence to convince even skeptical readers:

> When you think about it, it's impossible to lose — as many diets suggest — 10 pounds of *fat* in ten days, even on a total fast. A pound of body fat represents 3,500 calories. To lose 1 pound of fat, you must expend 3,500 more calories than you consume. Let's say you weigh 170 pounds and, as a moderately active person, you burn 2,500 calories a day. If your diet contains only 1,500 calories, you'd have an energy deficit of 1,000 calories a day. In a week's time that would add up to a 7,000-calorie deficit, or 2 pounds of real fat. In ten days, the accumulated deficit would

represent nearly 3 pounds of lost body fat. Even if you ate nothing at all for ten days and maintained your usual level of activity, your caloric deficit would add up to 25,000 calories.... At 3,500 calories per pound of fat, that's still only 7 pounds of lost fat.
　　　　　　　　　—Jane Brody, *Jane Brody's Nutrition Book*

Paragraph organization

Although paragraphs may be organized in almost infinitely many ways, certain patterns of organization occur frequently, either alone or in combination: examples and illustrations, process, comparison and contrast, cause and effect, classification, and definition. There is nothing magical about these patterns. They simply reflect the natural ways in which we think.

EXAMPLES AND ILLUSTRATIONS   Examples, perhaps the most common pattern of organization, are appropriate whenever the reader might be tempted to ask "For example?"

　　　A passenger list of the early years of the Orient Express would read like a *Who's Who of the World,* from art to politics. Sarah Bernhardt and her Italian counterpart Eleonora Duse used the train to thrill the stages of Europe. For musicians there were Toscanini and Mahler. Dancers Nijinsky and Pavlova were there, while lesser performers like Harry Houdini and the girls of the Ziegfeld Follies also rode the rails. Violinists were allowed to practice on the train, and occasionally one might see trapeze artists hanging like bats from the baggage racks.
　　　　　　　　　—Barnaby Conrad III, "Train of Kings"

Illustrations are extended examples, frequently presented in story form.

　　　Part of Harriet Tubman's strategy of conducting was, as in all battle-field operations, the knowledge of how and when to retreat. Numerous allusions have been made to her moves when she suspected that she was in danger. When she feared the party was closely pursued, she would take it for a time on a train southward bound. No one seeing Negroes going in this direction would for an instant suppose them to be fugitives. Once on her return she was at a railway station. She saw some men reading a poster and she heard one of them reading it aloud. It was a description of her, offering a reward for her capture. She took a southbound train to avert suspicion. At another time when Harriet heard men talking about her, she pretended to read a book which she carried. One man remarked, "This cannot be the woman. The one we want can't read or write." Harriet devoutly hoped the book was right side up.   —Earl Conrad, *Harriet Tubman*

PROCESS   A process paragraph is structured in chronological order. A writer may choose this pattern either to describe a process or to show readers how to follow a process.

> A presidential election in those days was neither simple nor direct. In each State the Electoral College voted for both offices, without designating which of the candidates was to get first place (the Presidency) and which second (the Vice-Presidency). The votes were then sent to the national capital to be counted. The candidate who had the highest number of votes was declared President and the next highest, Vice-President. If the two leading candidates had an equal number of votes, the election was to be decided in the House of Representatives, wherein each State cast one vote. Communication being slow and uncertain, it took several weeks for all the votes to come in from States so far apart as Georgia and Massachusetts.   —Saul K. Padover, *Jefferson*

COMPARISON AND CONTRAST   To compare two subjects is to draw attention to their similarities, although the word *compare* also has a broader meaning that includes a consideration of differences. To contrast is to focus only on differences.

Whether a comparison-and-contrast paragraph stresses similarities or differences, it may be patterned in one of two ways. The two subjects may be presented one at a time, block style, as in the following paragraph of contrast.

> So Grant and Lee were in complete contrast, representing two diametrically opposed elements in American life. Grant was the modern man emerging; beyond him, ready to come on the stage, was the great age of steel and machinery, of crowded cities and a restless burgeoning vitality. Lee might have ridden down from the old age of chivalry, lance in hand, silken banner fluttering over his head. Each man was the perfect champion of his cause, drawing both his strengths and weaknesses from the people he led.
>   —Bruce Catton, "Grant and Lee: A Study in Contrasts"

Or a paragraph may proceed point by point, treating two subjects together, one aspect at a time. The following paragraph uses the point-by-point method to both compare and contrast.

Wilson brought qualities as unusual as those of Theodore
Roosevelt to American politics. The two men had much in common: cultivation, knowledge, literary skill, personal magnetism,
relentless drive. But, where Roosevelt was unbuttoned and expan-
sive, Wilson was reserved and cool; no one known to history ever
called him "Woody" or "W.W." Both were lay preachers, but where
Roosevelt was a revivalist, bullying his listeners to hit the saw-
dust trail, Wilson had the severe eloquence of a Calvinist divine.
Roosevelt's egotism overflowed his personality; Wilson's was a
hard concentrate within. Roosevelt's power lay in what he did,
Wilson's in what he held in reserve.

—Arthur M. Schlesinger, Jr.,
The Age of Roosevelt: The Crisis of the Old Order

CAUSE AND EFFECT   A paragraph may move from cause to effects
or from an effect to its causes. The topic sentence in the following
paragraph mentions an effect; the rest of the paragraph lists several
causes.

The fantastic water clarity of the Mount Gambier sinkholes
results from several factors. The holes are fed from aquifers holding rainwater that fell decades—even centuries—ago, and that
has been filtered through miles of limestone. The high level of cal-
cium that limestone adds causes the silty detritus from dead
plants and animals to cling together and settle quickly to the bottom. Abundant bottom vegetation in the shallow sinkholes also
helps bind the silt. And the rapid turnover of water prohibits
stagnation.

—Hillary Hauser, "Exploring a Sunken Realm in Australia"

CLASSIFICATION   Classification is the grouping of items into categories according to some consistent principle.

Considering the millions and millions of antiques that one
sees in London, it is surprising how little variety there is. A fairly
careful survey of several London antique markets suggests that
there are only eight basic items for sale. These are (1) the broken
clock; (2) the old map, usually of a place unlisted in the geogra-
phies, called Novum Cloacum; (3) the incomplete set of dining-
room chairs (commonly five or seven), one of which has a broken
rung; (4) the set of three silver spoons; (5) the cracked demi-tasse
with saucer; (6) the dining-room table with (Variation A) no
leaves or (Variation B) a dangerous split in one leg; (7) the oil
portrait of someone who, though unidentified, might very well be
the Electress Sophia of Hanover or King Umberto the First; and

(8) the first edition volume of a history of animal husbandry during the year 1703 in the environs of Dumfries.

—Russell Baker, *Poor Russell's Almanac*

DEFINITION   A definition puts a word or concept into a general
class and then provides enough details to distinguish it from other
members in the same class.

Paragraphs of definition frequently make use of other patterns
of development. In the following paragraph, for example, a number
of illustrations are used to define the typical teenage victim in a
"slasher" film.

> Since teenagers are the target audience for slasher films, the
> victims in the films are almost always independent, fun-loving,
> just-out-of-high school partygoers. The girls all love to take late-
> night strolls alone through the woods or to skinny-dip at midnight
> in a murky lake. The boys, eager to impress the girls, prove their
> manhood by descending alone into musty cellars to restart broken
> generators or by chasing psychotic killers into haylofts and attics.
> Entering dark and gloomy houses, young men and women alike
> decide suddenly that now's a good time to save a few bucks on the
> family's electric bill—so they leave the lights off. After hearing a
> noise within the house, they always foolishly decide to investigate,
> thinking it's one of their many missing friends or pets. Disregard-
> ing the "safety in numbers" theory, they branch off in separate di-
> rections, never to see each other again. Or the teenagers fall into
> the common slasher-movie habit of walking backward, which
> naturally leads them right into you-know-who. Confronted by the
> ax-wielding maniac, the senseless youths lose their will to sur-
> vive, close their eyes, and scream.
>
> —Matthew J. Holicek, a student

Paragraph coherence

When sentences and paragraphs flow from one to another without
discernible bumps, gaps, or shifts, they are said to be coherent. Coherence can be improved by strengthening the various ties between
old information and new. A number of techniques for strengthening
those ties are detailed in this section.

REPEATING KEY WORDS   Repetition of key words is an important
technique for gaining coherence. To prevent repetitions from becoming dull, you can use variations of the key word (*hike, hiker, hiking*),
pronouns referring to the word (*gamblers . . . they*), and synonyms

(*run, spring, race, dash*). In the following paragraph describing plots among indentured servants in the seventeenth century, historian Richard Hofstadter binds sentences together by repeating the key word *plots* and echoing it with a variety of synonyms (which are italicized).

> *Plots* hatched by several servants to run away together oc-
> curred mostly in the plantation colonies, and the few recorded
> servant *uprisings* were entirely limited to those colonies. Virginia
> had been forced from its very earliest years to take stringent
> steps against *mutinous plots,* and severe punishments for *such be-*
> *havior* were recorded. Most servant *plots* occurred in the seven-
> teenth century: a contemplated *uprising* was nipped in the bud in
> York County in 1661; apparently led by some left-wing offshoots
> of the *Great Rebellion,* servants *plotted* an *insurrection* in
> Gloucester County in 1663, and four leaders were condemned and
> executed; some discontented servants apparently joined *Bacon's*
> *Rebellion* in the 1670's. In the 1680's, the planters became newly
> apprehensive of discontent among the servants "owing to their
> great necessities and want of clothes," and it was feared that they
> would *rise up* and *plunder* the storehouses and ships; in 1682
> there were plant-cutting *riots* in which servants and laborers, as
> well as some planters, took part. [Italics added]
> —Richard Hofstadter, *America at 1750*

USING PARALLEL STRUCTURES Parallel structures are frequently used within sentences to underscore the similarity of ideas (see E1). They may also be used to bind together a series of sentences ex-pressing similar information. In the following passage describing folk beliefs, anthropologist Margaret Mead presents similar infor-mation in parallel grammatical form.

> Actually, almost everyday, even in the most sophisticated home,
> something is likely to happen that evokes the memory of some
> old folk belief. The salt spills. A knife falls to the floor. Your nose
> tickles. Then perhaps, with a slightly embarrassed smile, the
> person who spilled the salt tosses a pinch over his left shoulder.
> Or someone recites the old rhyme "Knife falls, gentleman calls." Or
> as you rub your nose you think, That means a letter. I wonder
> who's writing?   —Margaret Mead, "New Superstitions for Old"

PROVIDING TRANSITIONS Certain words and phrases signal con-nections between ideas, connections that might otherwise be missed. Frequently used transitions are included in the following list.

TO SHOW ADDITION
and, also, besides, further, furthermore, in addition, moreover, next, too, first, second

TO GIVE EXAMPLES
for example, for instance, to illustrate, in fact, specifically

TO COMPARE
also, in the same manner, similarly, likewise

TO CONTRAST
but, however, on the other hand, in contrast, nevertheless, still, even though, on the contrary, yet, although

TO SUMMARIZE OR CONCLUDE
in other words, in short, in summary, in conclusion, to sum up, that is, therefore

TO SHOW TIME
after, as, before, next, during, later, finally, meanwhile, then, when, while, immediately

TO SHOW PLACE OR DIRECTION
above, below, beyond, farther on, nearby, opposite, close, to the left

TO INDICATE LOGICAL RELATIONSHIP
if, so, therefore, consequently, thus, as a result, for this reason, since

Skilled writers use transitional expressions with care, making sure, for example, not to use a *consequently* when an *also* would be more precise. They are also careful to select transitions with an appropriate tone, perhaps preferring *so* to *thus* in an informal piece, *in summary* to *in short* for a scholarly essay.

In the following paragraph, taken from an argument that dinosaurs had the " 'right-sized' brains for reptiles of their body size," biologist Stephen Jay Gould uses transitions (italicized) with skill:

> I don't wish to deny that the flattened, minuscule head of the large bodied "Stegosaurus" houses little brain from our subjective, top-heavy perspective, *but* I do wish to assert that we should not expect more of the beast. *First of all,* large animals have relatively smaller brains than related, small animals. The correlation of brain size with body size among kindred animals (all reptiles, all mammals, *for example*) is remarkably regular. *As* we move from small to large animals, from mice to elephants *or* small lizards to Komodo dragons, brain size increases, *but* not so fast as

body size. *In other words,* bodies grow faster than brains, *and* large animals have low ratios of brain weight to body weight. *In fact,* brains grow only about two-thirds as fast as bodies. *Since* we have no reason to believe that large animals are consistently stupider than their smaller relatives, we must conclude that large animals require relatively less brain to do as well as smaller animals. *If* we do not recognize this relationship, we are likely to underestimate the mental power of very large animals, dinosaurs in particular. [Italics added]

—Stephen Jay Gould, "Were Dinosaurs Dumb?"

MAINTAINING CONSISTENCY   Coherence suffers whenever a draft shifts confusingly from one point of view to another or from one verb tense to another (see E4).

Paragraph length

Ideally, paragraphs reflect the organization of the essay: one paragraph per point in short essays, a group of paragraphs per point in longer ones. Some ideas require more development than others, however, so it is best to be flexible. If an idea stretches to a length unreasonable for a paragraph, it should be divided, even if comparable points in the essay have been presented in single paragraphs.

Most readers feel comfortable with paragraphs ranging between 100 and 200 words. Shorter paragraphs force too much starting and stopping, and longer ones strain the reader's attention span. There are exceptions to this general rule, however. Paragraphs longer than 200 words frequently appear in scholarly writing, where they suggest seriousness and depth. Paragraphs shorter than 100 words occur in newspapers because of narrow columns; in informal essays to quicken the pace; and in business letters, where information is routinely scanned.

C2-c Draft a conclusion.

The conclusion should echo your main idea, without dully repeating it. Often the concluding paragraph can be relatively short.

In addition to echoing your main idea, a conclusion might summarize your main point, pose a question for future study, offer advice, or propose a course of action. To end an essay detailing the social skills required of a bartender, one writer concludes with some advice:

> If someone were to approach me one day looking for the se-
> cret to running a good bar, I suppose I would offer the following
> advice: Get your customers to pour out their ideas at a greater
> rate than you pour out the liquor. You will both win in the end.
> —Kathleen Lewis

To make the conclusion memorable, consider including a detail, example, or image from the introduction to bring readers full circle; a quotation or bit of dialogue; an anecdote; or a humorous, witty, or ironic comment.

Whatever concluding strategy you choose, avoid introducing new ideas at the end of an essay. Also avoid apologies and other limp, indeterminate endings. You should end crisply, preferably on a positive note.

C3

Revising

For the experienced writer, revising is rarely a one-step process. The larger elements of writing generally receive attention first — the focus, organization, paragraphing, content, and overall strategy. Improvements in sentence structure, word choice, grammar, punctuation, and mechanics come later.

C3-a Make global revisions.

Global revisions address the larger elements of writing. Usually they affect chunks of text longer than a sentence, and frequently they can be quite dramatic. Whole paragraphs might be dropped, others added. Material once stretched over two or three paragraphs might be condensed into one. Entire sections might be rearranged. Even the content may change dramatically, for the process of revising stimulates thought.

Many of us resist global revisions because we find it difficult to distance ourselves from a draft. We tend to review our work from our own, not from our audience's, perspective.

To distance yourself from a draft, put it aside for a while, preferably overnight or even longer. When you return to it, try to play the role of your audience as you read. If possible, enlist the help of reviewers — persons willing to play the role of audience for you. Ask your reviewers to focus on the larger issues of writing, not on the fine points. The following checklist may help them get started.

Checklist for global revision

Purpose and audience

1. Does the draft accomplish its purpose — to inform readers, to persuade them, to entertain them, to call them to action (or some combination of these)?
2. Is the draft appropriate for its audience? Does it take into consideration the audience's knowledge of the subject, level of interest in the subject, and possible attitudes toward the subject?
3. Is the level of formality appropriate?
4. Is the reading level appropriate?

Focus and organization

5. Do the introduction and conclusion focus clearly on the main point?
6. Can readers follow the overall structure?
7. Are ideas ordered effectively?

Content

8. Is the supporting material persuasive?
9. Which ideas need further development?
10. Are the parts proportioned sensibly? Do major ideas receive enough attention?
11. Where might material be deleted?

Paragraphs

12. Is each body paragraph unified, adequately developed, organized, and coherent?
13. Are any paragraphs too long or too short for easy reading?

C3-b Revise and edit sentences.

Most of the rest of this book offers advice on revising sentences for style and clarity and on editing them for grammar, punctuation, and mechanics. The process of revising and editing sentences should ordinarily occur right on the pages of an earlier draft, like this:

> ~~Finally we decided~~ *deciding* that perhaps our dream needed ~~some~~ prompting, ~~and~~ we visited a fertility doctor and began the expensive, time–consuming round of proce-
> dures that held out *some* ~~the~~ promise of ~~fulfilling our~~ *our dream's fulfillment. Our*
> ~~dream. All this was~~ *efforts, however, were* to no avail*,* ~~and as~~ *As* we approached
> the sixth year of our marriage, we ~~had reached the~~ *could no longer*
> ~~point where we couldn't~~ even discuss our childlessness
> without becoming very depressed. We questioned why
> this had happened to us~~?~~*.* Why had we been singled out
> for *such a* ~~this~~ major disappointment?

The original paragraph was flawed by wordiness and an excessive reliance on structures connected with *and*. Such problems can be addressed through any number of acceptable revisions. The first sentence, for example, could have been changed like this:

> Finally we decided that perhaps our dream needed
> ~~some~~ prompting*.* *After visiting* ~~and we visited~~ a fertility doctor*,* *we* ~~and~~
> began the expensive, time–consuming round of proce-
> dures that *promised hope* ~~held out the promise~~ of fulfilling our
> dream.

Though some writers might argue about the effectiveness of these improvements compared with the previous revision, most would agree that both revisions are better than the original.

Some of the paragraph's improvements involve less choice and are not so open to debate. The hyphen in *time-consuming* is necessary; a noun must be substituted for the pronoun *this,* which was being used more loosely than grammar allows; and the question mark in the next-to-last sentence must be changed to a period.

As it details the various rules for revising and editing sentences, this reference book suggests when an improvement is simply one among several possibilities and when it is more strictly a matter of right and wrong.

C4

Working on a word processor

A word processor, as you probably know, is a computer equipped with software that allows writers to compose and revise text with ease. Although a word processor cannot think for you, it can be a useful tool at all stages of the writing process: planning, drafting, and revising.

C4-a Planning

You can list or "brainstorm" ideas as easily on a word processor as with pencil and paper, especially if you are a fast typist. Later you can delete ideas, add others, and rearrange the order, all with a few keystrokes. And as you begin to perceive relationships among ideas, you may be able to turn your list into an informal outline.

Outlines can be created on a word processor quite easily. Some software packages will generate a formal outline structure for you — not the words, of course, but the conventional system of numbers and letters at appropriate indent levels.

If you like to begin a writing task by asking yourself questions, consider keeping sets of questions on file in your computer. A college student, for example, might use one set of questions for writing about literature, another for science reports, another for case studies in sociology or psychology, and so on. In some disciplines, sets of questions have been developed on software by experts in the field. Check with a professor or with your school's writing center to learn about such computer programs.

Software has also been developed to speed the process of academic research. Instead of taking notes on note cards, you can type notes on the computer, code them to reflect the divisions of your outline, and later print the notes in sorted batches. To rearrange the notes, you simply change their codes.

Although the computer can be a useful tool for planning, its advantages over pencil and paper should not be overstated. Not all planning techniques can be done on a word processor (clustering and branching cannot, for example), and a computer will not always be available when an idea strikes. Many writers find that they plan just as easily with pencil and paper; they turn to the computer primarily for drafting and revising.

C4-b Drafting

Whether to write a first draft on a word processor is a matter of personal preference. Some writers prefer the sensation of a pencil or pen moving on paper; others like to get their fingers moving on a keyboard.

One advantage of drafting at a keyboard, if you are a good typist, is speed: Your thoughts are not likely to race ahead of your fingers, as they sometimes do when you are drafting by hand. Another advantage is readability. As you draft, you will find yourself reviewing from time to time what you have already written. Typed copy — whether on a screen or printed out on paper — is easier to read than most handwriting.

A third advantage is flexibility. Because changes are so easy to make, a word processor encourages experimentation. If you get stuck while writing the opening paragraph, for example, you can skip ahead, knowing that it will be easy to insert the introduction later. Or you can switch screens and use an empty screen for brainstorming. Or if you have a creative but unusual idea for the introduction, you can try it out, confident that if you don't like it, you can make it disappear in seconds.

If you decide to type an initial draft on a word processor, it's a good idea to print out hard copy as you go along so that you can easily review what you have written. (Otherwise you will need to scroll from screen to screen.) Once you are done, be sure to save your draft in the computer's memory before turning off the computer.

C4-c Revising

The word processor is an excellent tool for revision. As mentioned earlier, revising is nearly always a two-step process. Global revisions, those that affect blocks of text longer than a sentence, generally should be handled first. They include changes in focus, organization, paragraphing, and content. (See C3-a.) Sentence-level revisions — improvements in sentence structure, word choice, grammar, punctuation, and mechanics — can come later. (See C3-b.)

Global revisions

Let's assume that you have typed and saved your rough draft on a computer equipped with a word-processing package. You have printed a copy of the draft, reviewed it for global revisions, and marked it up to indicate where you need to add, delete, and move chunks of text.

Once you have called up the text onto the computer's screen, you move the cursor to the place where you want to add, delete, or move text. Most word-processing packages allow you to add text simply by typing it in and to delete text by hitting a delete key. Moving blocks of text is a bit more complicated, usually requiring several keystrokes, but with practice it too is relatively simple.

Because the computer saves time, it encourages you to experiment with global revisions. Should you combine two paragraphs? Would your conclusion make a good introduction? Might several paragraphs be rearranged for greater impact? Will boldface headings improve the readability? With little risk, you can explore the possibilities. When a revision misfires, it is easy to restore your original draft.

Sentence-level revisions

Some writers handle sentence-level revisions directly at the computer, but most prefer to print out a hard copy of the draft, mark it up, and then return to the computer. Once you've indicated changes on the hard copy, you can enter them into the computer in a matter of minutes.

Software can provide help with sentence-level revisions. Many word processing programs have spelling checkers that will catch most but not all spelling errors (see M5), and some have thesauruses to help with word choice. Other programs, called *text analyzers* or *style checkers*, will flag a variety of possible problems: wordiness, jargon, weak verbs, long sentences, and so on. Be aware, however, that a text analyzer can only point out *possible* problems. It can tell you that a sentence is long, for example, but you must decide whether your long sentence is effective.

To proofread your final text, either read the words on the screen or, if this is too hard on your eyes, print a new copy and proofread the hard copy. Enter any necessary corrections into the computer, print a final copy, and you are done. To preserve the final draft in the computer's memory, be sure to save it before you turn off the computer.

Grammatical
Sentences

G

Grammatical Sentences

G1

Subject-verb agreement

In the present tense, verbs agree with their subjects in number (singular or plural) and in person (first, second, or third). The present-tense ending -*s* is used on a verb if its subject is third-person singular; otherwise the verb takes no ending. Consider, for example, the present-tense forms of the verb *give:*

	SINGULAR	PLURAL
FIRST PERSON	I give	we give
SECOND PERSON	you give	you give
THIRD PERSON	he/she/it gives	they give
	Alison gives	parents give

The verb *be* varies from this pattern, and unlike any other verb it has special forms in *both* the present and the past tense.

PRESENT-TENSE FORMS OF BE		PAST-TENSE FORMS OF BE	
I am	we are	I was	we were
you are	you are	you were	you were
he/she/it is	they are	he/she/it was	they were

G1-a Make the verb agree with its subject, not with a word that comes between.

Word groups often come between the subject and the verb. Such word groups, usually modifying the subject, may contain a noun that at first appears to be the subject. By mentally stripping away such modifiers, you can isolate the noun that is in fact the subject.

The *tulips* in the pot on the balcony *need* watering.

▶ High levels of air pollution causes damage to the respiratory tract.

The subject is *levels,* not *pollution.* Strip away the phrase *of air pollution* to hear the correct verb: *levels cause.*

costs

▶ A good set of golf clubs ~~cost~~ about three hundred dollars.
                          ∧

The subject is *set,* not *clubs.* Strip away the phrase *of golf clubs* to hear the correct verb: *set costs.*

NOTE: Phrases beginning with the prepositions *as well as, in addition to, accompanied by, together with,* and *along with* do not make a singular subject plural.

▶ The governor, as well as his press secretary, ~~were~~ shot.
  was

To emphasize that two people were shot, the writer could use *and* instead: *The governor and his press secretary were shot.*

G1-b Treat most compound subjects connected by *and* as plural.

A subject with two or more parts is said to be compound. If the parts are connected by *and,* the subject is nearly always plural.

Leon and *Jan* often *jog* together.

▶ Jill's natural ability and her desire to help others ~~has~~ led to a
  have

career in the ministry.

EXCEPTIONS: When the parts of the subject form a single unit or when they refer to the same person or thing, treat the subject as singular.

Strawberries and cream was a last-minute addition to the menu.

Sue's friend and adviser was surprised by her decision.

When a compound subject is preceded by *each* or *every,* treat the subject as singular.

Each tree, shrub, and vine needs to be sprayed.

G1-c With compound subjects connected by *or* or *nor,* make the verb agree with the part of the subject nearer to the verb.

A driver's *license* or credit *card is* required.

A driver's *license* or two credit *cards are* required.

▶ If a relative or neighbor ~~are~~ abusing a child, notify the police.
  is

> *were*
> ▶ Neither the instructor nor her students ~~was~~ able to find the
>
> classroom.

G1-d Treat most indefinite pronouns as singular.

Indefinite pronouns refer to nonspecific persons or things. Even though the following indefinite pronouns may seem to have plural meanings, treat them as singular in formal English: *anybody, anyone, each, either, everybody, everyone, everything, neither, none, no one, someone, something*.

> *Everyone* on the team *supports* the coach.

> *has*
> ▶ Each of the furrows ~~have~~ been seeded.

> *requires*
> ▶ None of these trades ~~require~~ a college education.

A few indefinite pronouns (*all, any, some*) may be singular or plural depending on the noun or pronoun they refer to.

> *Some* of the *lemonade has* disappeared.

> *Some* of the *rocks were* slippery.

G1-e Treat collective nouns as singular unless the meaning is clearly plural.

Collective nouns such as *jury, committee, audience, crowd, class, troop, family,* and *couple* name a class or a group. In American English collective nouns are usually treated as singular: They emphasize the group as a unit. Occasionally, when there is some reason to draw attention to the individual members of the group, a collective noun may be treated as plural.

> SINGULAR   The *class respects* the teacher.

> PLURAL   The *class are* debating among themselves.

To underscore the notion of individuality in the second sentence, many writers would add a clearly plural noun such as *members: The members of the class are debating among themselves.*

▶ The scout troop ~~meet~~ *meets* in our basement on Tuesdays.

The troop as a whole meets in the basement; there is no reason to draw attention to its individual members.

▶ A young couple ~~was~~ *were* arguing about politics while holding hands.

The meaning is clearly plural. Only individuals can argue and hold hands.

NOTE: The phrase *the number* is treated as singular, *a number* as plural.

SINGULAR   *The number* of school-age children *is* declining.

PLURAL   *A number* of children *are* attending the wedding.

NOTE: When units of measurement are used collectively, treat them as singular; when they refer to individual persons or things, treat them as plural.

SINGULAR   *Three-fourths* of the pie *has* been eaten.

PLURAL   *One-fourth* of the drivers *were* drunk.

G1-f Make the verb agree with its subject even when the subject follows the verb.

Verbs ordinarily follow subjects. When this normal order is reversed, it is easy to become confused. Sentences beginning with *there is* or *there are* (or *there was* or *there were*) are inverted; the subject follows the verb.

There *are* surprisingly few *children* in our neighborhood.

▶ There ~~was~~ *were* a social worker and a crew of twenty volunteers.

The subject *worker and crew* is plural, so the verb must be *were.*

NOTE: Occasionally a writer may invert a sentence for variety or effect.

▶ Behind the fence <del>is</del> *are* a fierce dog and an even fiercer cat.

The subject *dog and cat* is plural, so the verb must be *are*.

G1-g Make the verb agree with its subject, not with a subject complement.

One sentence pattern in English consists of a subject, a linking verb, and a subject complement: *Jack is an attorney.* (See R2-b.) Because the subject complement names or describes the subject, it is sometimes mistaken for the subject.

▶ A tent and a sleeping bag <del>is</del> *are* the required equipment.

Tent and bag is the subject, not *equipment.*

▶ A major force in today's economy <del>are</del> *is* women — as earners, consumers, and investors.

Force is the subject, not *women.* If the correct sentence seems awkward, you can make *women* the subject: *Women are a major force. . . .*

G1-h *Who, which,* and *that* take verbs that agree with their antecedents.

Like most pronouns, the relative pronouns *who, which,* and *that* have antecedents, nouns or pronouns to which they refer. Relative pronouns used as subjects of subordinate clauses take verbs that agree with their antecedents.

Take a *suit that travels* well.

Problems arise with the constructions *one of the* and *only one of the.* As a rule, treat *one of the* constructions as plural, *only one of the* constructions as singular.

▶ Our ability to use language is one of the things that sets us apart from animals.

The antecedent of *that* is *things,* not *one.* Several things set us apart from animals.

▶ Dr. Barker knew that Frank was the only one of his sons who
was
~~were~~ responsible enough to handle the estate.
^

The antecedent of *who* is *one,* not *sons.* Only one son was responsible enough.

G1-i Words such as *athletics, economics, mathematics, physics, statistics, measles,* and *news* are usually singular, despite their plural form.

▶ Statistics ~~are~~
is
^ among the most difficult courses in our program.

EXCEPTION: When the meaning is clearly plural, words ending in *-ics* are treated as plural: *The statistics are impressive.*

G1-j Titles of works and words mentioned as words are singular.

▶ *Lost Cities* ~~describe~~
describes
^ the discoveries of many ancient civilizations.

▶ *Controlled substances* ~~are~~
is
^ a euphemism for illegal drugs.

G2

Other problems with verbs

The verb is the heart of the sentence, so it is important to get it right. Section G1 deals with the problem of subject-verb agreement. This section describes a number of other potential problems with verbs.

G2-a Use the correct forms of irregular verbs.

Verbs have three principal forms: the infinitive, the past tense, and the past participle. The infinitive is the form listed in the dictionary. The past-tense form, which never has a helping verb, expresses action that occurred entirely in the past. The past participle is used with a helping verb, either with *has, have,* or *had* to form one of the perfect tenses (see G2-c) or with *be, am, is, are, was, were, being,* or *been* to form the passive voice (see G2-e).

INFINITIVE	We usually *go* to the beach in July.
PAST TENSE	Last July, we *went* to Paris.
PAST PARTICIPLE	We have *gone* to Paris twice.

For all regular verbs, the past-tense and past-participle forms are the same, ending in *-ed* or *-d,* so there is no danger of confusion (see R1-c). This is not true, however, for irregular verbs, such as the following:

INFINITIVE	PAST TENSE	PAST PARTICIPLE
begin	began	begun
fly	flew	flown
ride	rode	ridden

A list of irregular verbs begins on page 36.

In nonstandard speech, the past-tense and past-participle forms often differ from those of standard speech and writing.

▶ Yesterday we ~~seen~~ *saw* an unidentified flying object.

Because there is no helping verb, the past-tense form *saw* is required.

▶ The teacher asked Dwain if he had ~~did~~ *done* his homework.

Because of the helping verb *had,* the past-participle form *done* is required.

When in doubt about the standard English forms of irregular verbs, consult the following list or look up the infinitive form of the verb in the dictionary, which also lists irregular forms. (If no additional forms are listed in the dictionary, the verb is regular, not irregular.)

Common irregular verbs

INFINITIVE	PAST TENSE	PAST PARTICIPLE
arise	arose	arisen
awake	awoke	awaked
be	was, were	been
beat	beat	beaten, beat
become	became	become
begin	began	begun
bend	bent	bent
bite	bit	bitten, bit
blow	blew	blown
break	broke	broken
bring	brought	brought
build	built	built
burst	burst	burst
buy	bought	bought
catch	caught	caught
choose	chose	chosen
cling	clung	clung
come	came	come
cost	cost	cost
deal	dealt	dealt
dig	dug	dug
dive	dived, dove	dived
do	did	done
drag	dragged	dragged
draw	drew	drawn
dream	dreamed, dreamt	dreamed, dreamt
drink	drank	drunk
drive	drove	driven
drown	drowned	drowned
eat	ate	eaten
fall	fell	fallen
fight	fought	fought
find	found	found
fly	flew	flown
forget	forgot	forgotten, forgot
freeze	froze	frozen
get	got	gotten, got
give	gave	given
go	went	gone
grow	grew	grown
hang (suspend)	hung	hung
hang (execute)	hanged	hanged
have	had	had
hear	heard	heard

INFINITIVE	PAST TENSE	PAST PARTICIPLE
hide	hid	hidden
hurt	hurt	hurt
keep	kept	kept
know	knew	known
lay (put)	laid	laid
lead	led	led
lend	lent	lent
let (allow)	let	let
lie (recline)	lay	lain
lose	lost	lost
make	made	made
prove	proved	proved, proven
read	read	read
ride	rode	ridden
ring	rang	rung
rise (get up)	rose	risen
run	ran	run
say	said	said
see	saw	seen
send	sent	sent
set (place)	set	set
shake	shook	shaken
shoot	shot	shot
shrink	shrank	shrunk, shrunken
sing	sang	sung
sink	sank	sunk
sit (be seated)	sat	sat
slay	slew	slain
sleep	slept	slept
speak	spoke	spoken
spin	spun	spun
spring	sprang	sprung
stand	stood	stood
steal	stole	stolen
sting	stung	stung
strike	struck	struck, stricken
swear	swore	sworn
swim	swam	swum
swing	swung	swung
take	took	taken
teach	taught	taught
throw	threw	thrown
wake	woke, waked	waked, woken
wear	wore	worn
wring	wrung	wrung
write	wrote	written

G2-b Distinguish among the forms of *lie* and *lay.*

Writers and speakers frequently confuse the various forms of *lie* (meaning to recline or rest on a surface) and *lay* (meaning to put or place something). *Lie* is an intransitive verb; it does not take a direct object: *The tax forms lie on the table.* The verb *lay* is transitive; it takes a direct object: *Please lay the tax forms on the table.* (See R2-b.)

In addition to confusing the meaning of *lie* and *lay,* writers and speakers are often unfamiliar with the standard English forms of these verbs.

INFINITIVE	PAST TENSE	PAST PARTICIPLE	PRESENT PARTICIPLE
lie	lay	lain	lying
lay	laid	laid	laying

▶ Sue was so exhausted that she ~~laid~~ *lay* down for a nap.

The past-tense form of *lie* (to recline) is *lay.*

▶ Mary ~~lay~~ *laid* the baby on my lap.

The past-tense form of *lay* (to place) is *laid.*

▶ My grandmother's letters were ~~laying~~ *lying* in the corner of the chest.

The present participle of *lie* (to rest on a surface) is *lying.*

G2-c Choose the appropriate verb tense.

Tenses indicate the time of an action in relation to the time of the speaking or writing about that action.

The most common problem with tenses — shifting from one tense to another — is discussed in E4. Other problems with tenses are detailed in this section, after the following survey of tenses.

Survey of tenses

Tenses are classified as present, past, and future, with simple, perfect, and progressive forms for each.

The simple tenses indicate relatively simple time relations. The present tense is used primarily for actions occurring at the time of the speaking or for actions occurring regularly. The past tense is used for actions completed in the past. The future tense is used for actions that will occur in the future. In the following chart, the simple tenses are given for the regular verb *walk,* the irregular verb *ride,* and the highly irregular verb *be.*

PRESENT TENSE

SINGULAR		PLURAL	
I	walk, ride, am	we	walk, ride, are
you	walk, ride, are	you	walk, ride, are
he/she/it	walks, rides, is	they	walk, ride, are

PAST TENSE

SINGULAR		PLURAL	
I	walked, rode, was	we	walked, rode, were
you	walked, rode, were	you	walked, rode, were
he/she/it	walked, rode, was	they	walked, rode, were

FUTURE TENSE

I, you, he/she/it, we, they   will walk, ride, be

More complex time relations are indicated by the perfect and progressive tenses. A verb in one of the perfect tenses (a form of *have* plus the past participle) expresses an action that was or will be completed at the time of another action. A verb in a progressive tense (a form of *be* plus the present participle) expresses a continuing action.

PRESENT PERFECT

I, you, we, they	have walked, ridden, been
he/she/it	has walked, ridden, been

PAST PERFECT

I, you, he/she/it, we, they	had walked, ridden, been

FUTURE PERFECT

I, you, he/she/it, we, they	will have walked, ridden, been

PRESENT PROGRESSIVE

I	am walking, riding, being
he/she/it	is walking, riding, being
you, we, they	are walking, riding, being

PAST PROGRESSIVE

I, he/she/it	was walking, riding, being
you, we, they	were walking, riding, being

FUTURE PROGRESSIVE

I, you, he/she/it, we, they	will be walking, riding, being

Special uses of the present tense

Use the present tense when writing about literature or when expressing general truths.

When writing about a work of literature, you may be tempted to use the past tense. The convention, however, is to describe fictional events in the present tense.

▶ In Masuji Ibuse's *Black Rain,* a child ~~reached~~ *reaches* for a pomegranate in his mother's garden, and a moment later he ~~was~~ *is* dead, killed by the blast of the atomic bomb.

Scientific principles or general truths should appear in the present tense, unless such principles have been disproved.

▶ Galileo taught that the earth ~~revolved~~ *revolves* around the sun.

The past perfect tense

The past perfect tense is used for an action already completed by the time of another past action. This tense consists of a past participle preceded by *had (had worked, had gone).*

▶ We built our cabin high on a pine knoll, forty feet above an abandoned quarry that ~~was~~ *had been* flooded in 1920 to create a lake.

The building of the cabin and the flooding of the quarry both occurred in the past, but the flooding happened before the building.

G2-d Use verbs in the correct mood.

There are three moods in English: the indicative, used for facts, opinions, and questions; the imperative, used for orders or advice; and the subjunctive, used for wishes or conditions contrary to fact. Of these three moods, the subjunctive is most likely to cause problems.

In the subjunctive mood, present-tense verbs do not change form to indicate the number and person of the subject (see G1). Instead, all subjects of present-tense verbs take the infinitive verb form (*be, drive, employ*). Also, in the subjunctive mood there is only one past-tense form of *be: were* (never *was*).

Use the subjunctive mood in *if* clauses expressing conditions contrary to fact.

▶ If I ~~was~~ *were* a member of Congress, I would vote for the bill.

Use the subjunctive mood in *that* clauses following verbs such as *ask, insist, recommend, request,* and *wish*.

▶ Professor Moore insists that her students ~~are~~ *be* on time.

▶ Don't you wish that Janet ~~was~~ *were* here to help us celebrate?

G2-e Prefer the active voice.

Transitive verbs appear in either the active or the passive voice. (See R2-b.) In the active voice, the subject of the sentence does the action; in the passive, the subject receives the action. Although both voices are grammatically correct, the active voice is usually more effective because it is simpler and more direct.

ACTIVE   The committee *reached* a decision.

PASSIVE   A decision *was reached* by the committee.

To transform a sentence from the passive voice to the active voice, make the actor the subject of the sentence.

▶ For the opening flag ceremony, ~~a dance was choreographed by~~ Mr. Martins *choreographed a dance* to the song "Two Hundred Years and Still a Baby."

The passive voice is appropriate if you wish to emphasize the receiver of the action or to minimize the importance of the actor.

APPROPRIATE   As the time for harvest approaches, the tobacco
PASSIVE   plants *are sprayed* with a chemical to retard the
              growth of suckers.

The writer wished to focus on the tobacco plants, not on the people spraying them.

G3

Problems with pronouns

Pronouns are words that substitute for nouns (see R1-b). Four frequently encountered problems with pronouns are discussed in this section:

a.   pronoun-antecedent agreement (singular vs. plural)
b.   pronoun reference (clarity)
c.   pronoun case (personal pronouns such as *I* vs. *me, she* vs. *her*)
d.   pronoun case (*who* vs. *whom*)

For other problems with pronouns, consult the Glossary of Usage (W1).

G3-a Make pronouns and antecedents agree.

The antecedent of a pronoun is the word the pronoun refers to. A pronoun and its antecedent agree when they are both singular or both plural.

> SINGULAR   The *doctor* finished *her* rounds.
>
> PLURAL   The *doctors* finished *their* rounds.

Indefinite pronouns

Indefinite pronouns refer to nonspecific persons or things. Even though the following indefinite pronouns may seem to have plural meanings, treat them as singular in formal English: *anybody, anyone, each, either, everybody, everyone, everything, neither, none, no one, someone, something.*

> In this class everyone performs at his or her [*not* their] fitness level.

When a plural pronoun refers mistakenly to a singular indefinite pronoun, you will usually have three options for revision:

1. Replace the plural pronoun with *he or she* (or *his or her*);
2. make the antecedent plural;
3. or rewrite the sentence so that no problem of agreement arises.

▶ When someone has been drinking, ~~they are~~ more likely to speed.

he or she is

▶ When ~~someone has~~ been drinking, they are more likely to speed.

drivers have

▶ ~~When someone~~ has been drinking, ~~they are~~ more likely to speed.

Someone who   *is*

Because the *he or she* construction is wordy, often the second or third revision strategy is more effective.

NOTE: The traditional use of *he* (or *his*) to refer to persons of either sex is now widely considered as sexist (see W3-e).

Generic nouns

A generic noun represents a typical member of a group, such as a typical student, or any member of a group, such as any lawyer. Although generic nouns may seem to have plural meanings, they are singular.

> Every runner must train rigorously if he or she wants [*not* they want] to excel.

When a plural pronoun refers mistakenly to a generic noun, you will usually have three options for revision:

1. Replace the plural pronoun with *he or she* (or *his or her*);
2. make the antecedent plural;
3. or rewrite the sentence so that no problem of agreement arises.

▶ A medical student must study hard if ~~they want~~ to succeed.

he or she wants

▶ ~~A medical student~~ must study hard if they want to succeed.

Medical students

▶ A medical student must study hard ~~if they want~~ to succeed.

in order

Collective nouns

Collective nouns such as *jury, committee, audience, crowd, class, troop, family, team,* and *couple* name a class or group. If the group functions as a unit, as is usually the case, treat the collective noun as singular; if the members of the group function individually, treat the collective noun as plural.

AS A UNIT   The *committee* granted *its* permission to build.

AS INDIVIDUALS   The *committee* put *their* signatures on the document.

When treating a collective noun as plural, many writers prefer to add a clearly plural antecedent such as *members* to the sentence: *The members of the committee put their signatures on the document.*

To some extent, you can choose whether to treat a collective noun as singular or plural, depending on your meaning. Make sure, however, that you are consistent.

▶ The jury has reached their decision.

The writer selected the verb *has* to match the singular noun *jury* (see G1), so for consistency the pronoun must be *its*.

Compound antecedents

Treat compound antecedents joined by *and* as plural.

Joanne and John moved to the mountains, where *they* built a log cabin.

With compound antecedents joined by *or* or *nor,* make the pronoun agree with the nearer antecedent.

Either *Bruce* or *James* should receive first prize for *his* sculpture.

Neither the *instructor* nor her *students* could find *their* way to the bookstore.

If one of the antecedents is singular and the other plural, as in the second example, put the plural one last to avoid awkwardness.

G3-b Make pronoun references clear.

Pronouns substitute for nouns; they are a kind of shorthand. In a sentence like *After Andrew intercepted the ball, he kicked it as hard as he could,* the pronouns *he* and *it* substitute for the nouns *Andrew* and *ball.* The word a pronoun refers to is called its *antecedent.*

A pronoun should refer clearly to its antecedent. A pronoun's reference will be unclear if it is ambiguous, implied, vague, or indefinite.

Ambiguous reference

Ambiguous reference occurs when the pronoun could refer to two possible antecedents.

▶ When Gloria set the pitcher on the glass-topped table, ~~it~~ broke.   *the pitcher*

What broke—the table or the pitcher? The revision eliminates the ambiguity.

▶ Tom told James, *"You have* ~~that he had~~ won the lottery.*"*

Who won the lottery—Tom or James? The revision eliminates the ambiguity.

Implied reference

A pronoun must refer to a specific antecedent, not to a word that is implied but not present in the sentence.

▶ After braiding Ann's hair, Sue decorated ~~them~~ with ribbons.   *the braids*

The pronoun *them* referred to Ann's braids (implied by the term *braiding*), but the word *braids* did not appear in the sentence.

Modifiers, such as possessives, cannot serve as antecedents. A modifier may strongly imply the noun that the pronoun might logically refer to, but it is not itself that noun.

▶ In ~~Euripides'~~ *Medea*, ~~he~~ describes the plight of a woman rejected   *Euripides*

by her husband.

The pronoun *he* cannot refer logically to the possessive modifier *Euripides'*.

Vague reference of *this, that, or which*

The pronouns *this, that,* and *which* should not refer vaguely to earlier word groups or ideas. These pronouns should refer to specific antecedents. When a pronoun's reference is too vague, either replace the pronoun with a noun or supply an antecedent to which the pronoun clearly refers.

▶ More and more often, especially in large cities, we are finding ourselves victims of serious crimes. We learn to accept ~~this~~ with *our fate* minor complaints.

▶ Romeo and Juliet were both too young to have acquired much wisdom, which accounts for their rash actions. *a fact*

Indefinite reference of they, it, *or* you

The pronoun *they* should refer to a specific antecedent. Do not use *they* to refer indefinitely to persons who have not been specifically mentioned.

▶ Sometimes a list of ways to save energy is included with the gas bill. For example, ~~they suggest~~ setting a moderate temperature for the hot water heater. *the gas company suggests*

The word *it* should not be used indefinitely in constructions such as "In the article it says that...."

▶ ~~In~~ the report ~~it~~ points out that lifting the ban on Compound 1080, a long-lived pesticide, would prove detrimental to the bald eagle. *T*

The pronoun *you* is appropriate when the writer is addressing the reader directly: *Once you have kneaded the dough, let it rise in a warm place.* Except in very informal contexts, however, the indefinite *you* (meaning "anyone in general") is inappropriate.

▶ In Ethiopia, ~~you don't~~ need much property to be considered well off. *one doesn't*

If the pronoun *one* seems stilted, the writer might recast the sentence: *Ethiopians don't need much property to be considered well off.*

G3-c Use personal pronouns in the proper case.

The personal pronouns in the following chart change what is known as case form according to their grammatical function in a sentence. Pronouns functioning as subjects or subject complements appear in the *subjective* case; those functioning as objects appear in the *objective* case; and those functioning as possessives appear in the *possessive* case.

SUBJECTIVE CASE	OBJECTIVE CASE	POSSESSIVE CASE
I	me	my
we	us	our
you	you	your
he/she/it	him/her/it	his/her/its
they	them	their

This section explains the difference between the subjective and objective cases; then it alerts you to certain structures that may tempt you to choose the wrong pronoun. Finally, it describes a special use of possessive case pronouns.

Subjective case

When a pronoun functions as a subject or a subject complement, it must be in the subjective case (*I, we, you, he/she, they*).

SUBJECT	Sylvia and *he* shared the award.
SUBJECT COMPLEMENT	Greg announced that the winners were Sylvia and *he.*

Subject complements — words following linking verbs that complete the meaning of the subject — frequently cause problems for writers, since we rarely hear the correct form in casual speech. (See R2-b.)

▶ Sandra confessed that the artist was ~~her~~. *she*

The pronoun *she* follows the linking verb *was* and completes the meaning of the subject *artist.* If *artist was she* seems too stilted, try rewriting the sentence: *Sandra confessed that she was the artist.*

Objective case

When a pronoun functions as a direct object, an indirect object, or the object of a preposition, it must be in the objective case (*me, us, you, him/her, them*).

DIRECT OBJECT	Bruce found Tony and brought *him* home.
INDIRECT OBJECT	Alice gave *me* a surprise party.
OBJECT OF A PREPOSITION	Jessica wondered if the call was for *her*.

Compound word groups

When a subject or object appears as part of a compound structure, you may occasionally become confused. To test for the correct pronoun, mentally strip away all of the compound word group except the pronoun in question.

▶ Joel ran away from home because his stepfather and ~~him~~ *he* had

quarreled.

His stepfather and he is the subject of the verb *had quarreled*. If we strip away the words *his stepfather and*, the correct pronoun becomes clear: *he had quarreled* (not *him had quarreled*).

▶ Geoffrey went with my family and ~~I~~ *me* to King's Dominion.

Me is the object of the preposition *with*. We would not say *Geoffrey went with I*.

When in doubt about the correct pronoun, some writers try to evade the choice by using a reflexive pronoun such as *myself*. Such evasions are nonstandard, even though they are used by some educated persons.

▶ The Egyptian cab driver gave my husband and ~~myself~~ *me* some good

tips on traveling in North Africa.

My husband and me is the indirect object of the verb *gave*. For correct uses of *myself*, see the Glossary of Usage (W1).

Appositives

Appositives are noun phrases that rename nouns or pronouns. A pronoun in an appositive has the same function as the noun or pronoun it renames.

▶ At the drama festival, two actors, Christina and ~~me~~ *I*, were selected

to do the last scene of *King Lear*.

The appositive *Christina and I* renames the subject (*actors*).

▶ The college interviewed only two applicants for the job, Professor
Stevens and ~~I~~ *me*.

The appositive *Professor Stevens and me* renames the direct object (*applicants*).

We *or* us *before a noun*

When deciding whether *we* or *us* should precede a noun, choose the pronoun that would be appropriate if the noun were omitted.

▶ ~~Us~~ *We* tenants would rather fight than move.

▶ Management is short-changing ~~we~~ *us* tenants.

Comparisons with than *or* as

Sentence parts, usually verbs, are often omitted in comparisons beginning with *than* or *as*. To test for the correct pronoun, mentally complete the sentence.

▶ My husband is six years older than ~~me~~ *I*.

I is the subject of the verb *am*, which is understood. If the correct English seems too formal, add the verb: *My husband is six years older than I am.*

▶ We respected no other candidate as much as ~~she~~ *her*.

Her is the direct object of an understood verb: *We respected no other candidate as much as (we respected) her.*

Subjects of infinitives

An infinitive is the word *to* followed by a verb. Subjects of infinitives are an exception to the general rule that subjects must be in the subjective case. Whenever an infinitive has a subject, it must be in the objective case.

▶ We expected Chris and ~~he~~ *him* to win the doubles championship.

Chris and him is the subject of the infinitive *to win*.

Possessive case to modify a gerund

If a pronoun modifies a gerund or a gerund phrase, it should appear in the possessive case (*my, our, your, his/her/its, their*). A gerund is a verb form ending in *-ing* that functions as a noun. Gerunds frequently appear in phrases, in which case the whole gerund phrase functions as a noun. (See R3-c.)

▶ My father always tolerated ~~us~~ *our* talking after the lights were out.

The possessive pronoun *our* modifies the gerund *talking*.

Nouns as well as pronouns may modify gerunds. To form the possessive case of a noun, use an apostrophe and an *-s* (a victim's rights) or just an apostrophe (victims' rights). See P5-a.

▶ We had to pay a fifty-dollar fine for ~~Brenda~~ *Brenda's* driving without a permit.

The possessive noun *Brenda's* modifies the gerund phrase *driving without a permit*.

G3-d Use *who* and *whom* in the proper case.

Who, a subjective case pronoun, can be used only for subjects and subject complements. *Whom,* an objective case pronoun, can be used only for objects. (For more about pronoun case, see G3-c.)

Who and *whom* are relative pronouns used to introduce subordinate clauses. They are also interrogative pronouns used to open questions.

In subordinate clauses

The case of a relative pronoun in a subordinate clause is determined by its function *within the subordinate clause.*

▶ He tells that story to ~~whomever~~ *whoever* will listen.

Whoever is the subject of the subordinate clause *whoever will listen.* The object of the preposition *to* is the entire subordinate clause.

When it functions as an object in a subordinate clause, *whom* appears out of order, before both the subject and the verb. To choose the correct pronoun, you can mentally restructure the clause.

▶ You will work with our senior engineers, ~~who~~ *Whom* you will meet later.

Whom is the direct object of the verb of the subordinate clause. This becomes clear if we mentally restructure the clause: *you will meet whom.*

▶ The tutor ~~who~~ *whom* I was assigned to was very supportive.

Whom is the object of the preposition *to.* If the correct English seems too formal, drop the *whom: The tutor I was assigned to. . . .*

NOTE: Ignore inserted expressions such as *they know* or *I think* when determining the case of a relative pronoun.

▶ All of the school bullies want to take on a big guy ~~whom~~ *who* they

know won't hurt them.

Who is the subject of *won't hurt,* not the object of *know.*

In questions

The case of an interrogative pronoun is determined by its function within the question.

▶ ~~Whom~~ *Who* is responsible for this dastardly deed?

Who is the subject of the verb *is.*

When *whom* appears as an object in a question, it appears out of order, before both the subject and the verb. To choose the correct pronoun, you can mentally restructure the question.

▶ ~~Who~~ *Whom* did the committee select?

Whom is the direct object of the verb *did select:* The committee did select *whom?*

G4

Adjectives and adverbs

Adjectives modify nouns or pronouns; adverbs modify verbs, adjectives, or other adverbs. (See R1-d and R1-e.)

Many adverbs are formed by adding *-ly* to adjectives (*formal, formally*). But don't assume that all words ending in *-ly* are adverbs or that all adverbs end in *-ly*. Some adjectives end in *-ly* (*lovely, friendly*) and some adverbs don't (*always, here, there*). When in doubt, consult a dictionary.

G4-a Use adverbs, not adjectives, to modify verbs, adjectives, and adverbs.

When adverbs modify verbs (or verbals), they usually answer one of these questions: When? Where? How? Why? Under what conditions? How often? To what degree?

The incorrect use of adjectives in place of adverbs to modify verbs occurs primarily in casual or nonstandard speech.

▶ The arrangement worked out ~~perfect~~ *perfectly* for everyone.

The incorrect use of the adjective *good* in place of the adverb *well* is especially common in casual and nonstandard speech.

▶ I was surprised to hear that Louise had done so ~~good~~ *well* on the exam.

Adjectives are sometimes used incorrectly to modify adjectives or other adverbs.

▶ For a man eighty years old, Joe plays golf ~~real~~ *really* well.

G4-b Use adjectives, not adverbs, as subject complements.

Adjectives ordinarily precede nouns, but they can also function as subject complements following linking verbs (see R2-b). When an adjective functions as a subject complement, it describes the subject:

Justice is *blind*.

Problems can arise with verbs such as *smell, taste, look,* and *feel,* which may or may not be linking. If the word following one of these verbs describes the subject, use an adjective; if it modifies the verb, use an adverb.

ADJECTIVE   The detective looked *cautious*.

ADVERB   The detective looked *cautiously* for the fingerprints.

Linking verbs suggest states of being, not actions. For example, to look cautious suggests the state of being cautious, whereas to look cautiously is to perform an action in a cautious way.

▶ The lilacs in our backyard smell especially ~~sweetly~~ *sweet* this year.

▶ Lori looked ~~well~~ *good* in her new raincoat.

G4-c Use comparatives and superlatives with care.

Most adjectives and adverbs have three forms: the positive, the comparative, and the superlative.

POSITIVE	COMPARATIVE	SUPERLATIVE
soft	softer	softest
fast	faster	fastest
careful	more careful	most careful
bad	worse	worst
good	better	best

Comparative versus superlative

Use the comparative to compare two things, the superlative to compare three or more.

▶ Which of these two brands of toothpaste is ~~best~~? *better*

▶ Though Shaw and Jackson are impressive, Hobbs is the ~~more~~ *most* qualified of the three candidates running for mayor.

Form of comparatives and superlatives

To form comparatives and superlatives of most one- and two-syllable adjectives, use the endings -*er* and -*est*: *smooth, smoother, smoothest; easy, easier, easiest.* With longer adjectives, use *more* and *most* (or *less* and *least* for downward comparisons): *exciting, more exciting, most exciting; helpful, less helpful, least helpful.*

Some one-syllable adverbs take the endings -*er* and -*est* (*fast, faster, fastest*), but longer adverbs and all of those ending in -*ly* form the comparative and superlative with *more* and *most* (or *less* and *least*).

The comparative and superlative forms of the following adjectives and adverbs are irregular: *good, better, best; bad, worse, worst; badly, worse, worst.*

▶ The Kirov was the ~~superbest~~ ballet company we had ever seen. *most superb*

▶ Lloyd's luck couldn't have been ~~worser~~ than David's. *worse*

Double comparatives or superlatives

Do not use double comparatives or superlatives. When you have added -*er* or -*est* to an adjective or adverb, do not also use *more* or *most* (or *less* or *least*).

▶ Of all her family, Julia is the ~~most~~ happiest about the move.

▶ That is the most ~~vilest~~ joke I have ever heard. *vile*

Absolute concepts

Do not use comparatives or superlatives with absolute concepts such as *unique* or *perfect.* Either something is unique or it isn't. It is illogical to suggest that absolute concepts come in degrees.

▶ That is the most ~~unique~~ wedding gown I have ever seen. *unusual*

▶ The painting would have been even more ~~priceless~~ *valuable* had it been
signed.

G5

Sentence fragments

As a rule, do not treat a piece of a sentence as if it were a sentence.
To be a sentence, a word group must consist of at least one full
independent clause. An independent clause has a subject and a verb,
and it either stands alone or could stand alone.

This section shows you how to recognize the most common types
of fragments, and it suggests two revision strategies for each type.

G5-a Attach fragmented subordinate clauses or turn them into sentences.

A subordinate clause is patterned like a sentence, with both a subject and verb, but it begins with a word that tells readers it cannot
stand alone — a word such as *after, although, because, before, if,
though, unless, until, when, where, who, which,* and *that.* (See R3-e.)

Most fragmented clauses beg to be pulled into a sentence
nearby.

▶ Jane promises to address the problem of limited on-campus
parking / ~~If~~ *if* she is elected special student adviser.

If a fragmented clause cannot be attached to a nearby sentence
or if you feel that attaching it would be awkward, try rewriting it.
The simplest way to turn a subordinate clause into a sentence is to
delete the opening word or words that mark it as subordinate.

▶ Violence has produced a great deal of apprehension among
students and teachers. ~~So that self-preservation~~ *Self-preservation*, in fact, has
become their primary aim.

G5-b Attach fragmented phrases or turn them into sentences.

Like subordinate clauses, certain phrases are sometimes mistaken for sentences. For example, verbal phrases contain verb forms such as *swimming* or *to swim,* but because these verb forms are not really verbs, verbal phrases cannot stand alone (see R3-b). Frequently a fragmented verbal phrase may simply be attached to a nearby sentence.

▶ On Sundays James read the newspaper's employment sections
scrupulously*,* ~~Scrutinizing~~ *scrutinizing* every position that held even the
remotest possibility.

If the fragmented verbal phrase cannot be attached to a nearby sentence, try rewriting it.

▶ If Eric doesn't get his way, he goes into a fit of rage. For example,
~~lying~~ *he lies* on the floor screaming or ~~opening~~ *opens* the cabinet doors and then
~~slamming~~ *slams* them shut.

Appositive phrases — word groups that rename nouns or pronouns — are sometimes mistaken for sentences (see R3-c). To correct such a fragment, you can nearly always attach it to a nearby sentence.

▶ Wednesday morning Phil allowed himself half a grapefruit*,* *t*he only food he had eaten in two days.

G5-c Attach other fragmented word groups or turn them into sentences.

Other word groups that are commonly fragmented are parts of compound predicates and lists.

A predicate consists of a verb and its objects, complements, and modifiers (see R2). A compound predicate includes two or more predicates joined by a coordinating conjunction, usually *and, but,* or *or.* Because the parts of a compound predicate share the same subject, they should appear in the same sentence.

▶ Aspiring bodybuilders must first ascertain their strengths and

weaknesses/ And then develop a clear picture of what they want

to achieve.

The writer might also correct the fragment by turning the second predicate into a sentence: *They must then develop a clear picture of what they want to achieve.*

When a list is mistakenly fragmented, it can often be attached to a nearby sentence with a colon or a dash. (See P4 and P5.)

▶ The side effects of lithium are many/: Nausea, stomach cramps,

thirst, muscle weakness, vomiting, diarrhea, confusion, and

tremors.

G5-d Exception: Fragments may be used for special purposes.

Skilled writers occasionally use sentence fragments for the following special purposes:

FOR EMPHASIS	Following the dramatic Americanization of their children, even my parents grew more publicly confident. *Especially my mother.* —Richard Rodriguez
TO ANSWER A QUESTION	Are these new drug tests 100 percent reliable? *Not in the opinion of most experts.*
AS A TRANSITION	*And now the opposing arguments.*
EXCLAMATIONS	*Not again!*
IN ADVERTISING	*Fewer calories. Improved taste.*

Although fragments are sometimes appropriate, writers and readers do not always agree on when they are appropriate. Therefore you will find it safer to write in complete sentences.

G6

Comma splices and fused sentences

Comma splices and fused sentences contain independent clauses that have been too weakly separated. (An independent clause is a word group that can stand alone as a sentence.) When a writer puts no mark of punctuation between independent clauses, the result is a fused sentence:

┌─ INDEPENDENT CLAUSE ─┐ ┌─ INDEPENDENT CLAUSE ─┐

FUSED   Power tends to corrupt absolute power corrupts
absolutely.

A far more common error is the comma splice, which consists of independent clauses separated only by a comma:

COMMA   Power tends to corrupt, absolute power corrupts
SPLICE   absolutely.

If two independent clauses are to appear in one sentence, they must be firmly separated, either by a comma and a coordinating conjunction (*and, but, or, nor, for, so, yet*) or by a semicolon. (See P1-a and P3-a.)

REVISED   Power tends to corrupt, and absolute power corrupts
absolutely.

REVISED   Power tends to corrupt; absolute power corrupts
absolutely.

Even if the clauses are joined by a comma and a conjunctive adverb such as *moreover, however,* or *therefore,* the separation is still not firm enough. Clauses connected with a conjunctive adverb must be separated by a semicolon. (See P3-a.)

COMMA   Power tends to corrupt, moreover, absolute power
SPLICE   corrupts absolutely.

REVISED   Power tends to corrupt; moreover, absolute power
corrupts absolutely.

To correct a comma splice or a fused sentence, you will usually have four choices:

a. Use a comma and a coordinating conjunction.
b. Use a semicolon.
c. Make separate sentences.
d. Restructure the sentence.

One of these revision strategies will usually work better than the others for a particular sentence.

G6-a Consider separating the clauses with a comma and a coordinating conjunction.

There are seven coordinating conjunctions in English: *and, but, or, nor, for, so,* and *yet.* When a coordinating conjunction joins independent clauses, it must be preceded by a comma. (See P1-a.)

▶ Theo and Fanny had hoped to spend their final days in the old

homestead, _{but} they had to change their plans and move together to a

retirement home.

▶ Many government officials privately admit that the polygraph is

unreliable, _{yet} ~~however,~~ they continue to use it as a security measure.

G6-b Consider separating the clauses with a semicolon.

When the independent clauses are closely related and their relation is clear without a coordinating conjunction, a semicolon is an acceptable method of revision. (See P3.)

▶ Nicklaus is like fine wine; he gets better with time.

A semicolon is required between independent clauses that have been linked with a conjunctive adverb such as *however, therefore, moreover, furthermore,* or *nevertheless.*

▶ The timber wolf looks like a large German shepherd; however,

the wolf has longer legs, larger feet, a wider head, and a long,

bushy tail.

G6-c Consider making the clauses into separate sentences.

▶ In one episode viewers saw two people smashed by a boat, one

choked, and another shot to death. *What* ~~what~~ purpose does this

violence serve?

Since one independent clause is a statement and the other is a question, they should be separate sentences.

▶ I gave the necessary papers to the police officer. *T*hen he said I

would have to accompany him to the police station, where a

counselor would talk with me and call my parents.

Because the second independent clause is quite long, a sensible revision is to use separate sentences.

G6-d Consider restructuring the sentence, perhaps by subordinating one of the clauses.

If one of the independent clauses is less important than the other, try turning it into a subordinate clause or phrase. (See E6-a.)

▶ Lindsey is a top competitor *who* ~~she~~ has been riding since the age of

seven.

▶ *When the* ~~The~~ new health plan was explained to the employees in my

division, everyone agreed to give it a try.

▶ Saturday afternoon Julie came running into the house / ~~she~~

~~wanted~~ to get permission to go the the park.

Effective
Sentences

E

Effective Sentences

E1

Parallelism

If two or more ideas are parallel, they should be expressed in parallel grammatical form. Single words should be balanced with single words, phrases with phrases, clauses with clauses.

A kiss can be a comma, a question mark, or an exclamation point.
—Mistinguett

This novel is not to be tossed lightly aside, but to be hurled with great force. —Dorothy Parker

In matters of principle, stand like a rock; in matters of taste, swim with the current. —Thomas Jefferson

E1-a Balance parallel ideas linked with coordinating conjunctions.

Coordinating conjunctions (*and, but, or, nor, for, so, yet*) are used to connect a pair or a series of items. When those items are parallel in content, they should be expressed in parallel grammatical form.

▶ Theft, vandalism, and cheating can result in suspension or even ~~being expelled~~ *expulsion* from school.

The revision balances the noun *expulsion* with the noun *suspension*.

▶ Mary told the judge that she had been pulled out of a line of fast-moving traffic and ~~of her~~ *that she had a* perfect driving record.

A *that* clause is now paired with a *that* clause, not with an *of* phrase.

▶ David is responsible for stocking merchandise, ~~all in-store repairs,~~ *repairing items in the store,* writing orders for delivery, and ~~sales of~~ *selling* computers.

The revision uses *-ing* forms for all items in the series.

63

E1-b Balance parallel ideas linked with correlative conjunctions.

Correlative conjunctions come in pairs: *either . . . or, neither . . . nor, not only . . . but also, both . . . and, whether . . . or.* Make sure that the grammatical structure following the first half of the pair is the same as that following the second half.

▶ The shutters were not only too long but also ~~were~~ too wide.

> The words *too long* follow *not only,* so *too wide* should follow *but also.*

▶ I was advised either to change my flight or ^to^ take the train.

> *To change my flight,* which follows *either,* should be balanced with *to take the train,* which follows *or.*

E1-c Balance comparisons linked with *than* or *as.*

In comparisons linked with *than* or *as,* the elements being compared should appear in parallel grammatical structure.

▶ It is easier to speak in abstractions than ~~grounding~~ ^to ground^ one's thoughts in reality.

▶ Mother could not persuade me that giving is as much a joy as ~~to receive~~ ^receiving.^

NOTE: Comparisons should also be logical and complete. (See E2-c.)

E2

Needed words

Do not omit words necessary for grammatical or logical completeness. Readers need to see at a glance how the parts of a sentence are connected.

E2-a Add words needed to complete compound structures.

In compound structures, words are often omitted for economy: *Sam is a man who means what he says and [who] says what he means.* Such omissions are perfectly acceptable as long as the omitted word is common to both parts of the compound structure.

If the shorter version defies grammar or idiom because an omitted word is not common to both parts of the compound structure, the word must be put back in.

▶ Some of the regulars are acquaintances whom we see at work or *who*

live in our community.

The word *who* must be included because *whom live in our community* is not grammatically correct.

accepted
▶ I never have and never will accept a bribe.

Have . . . accept is not grammatically correct.

in
▶ Many of these tribes in the South Pacific still believe and live by

ancient laws.

Believe . . . by is not idiomatic English.

E2-b Add the word *that* if there is any danger of misreading without it.

If there is no danger of misreading, the word *that* may sometimes be omitted when it introduces a subordinate clause: *The value of a principle is the number of things [that] it will explain.* Occasionally, however, a sentence might be misread without the *that.*

that
▶ As Joe began to prepare dinner, he discovered the oven wasn't

working properly.

Joe didn't discover the oven; he discovered that the oven wasn't working properly.

E2-c Add words needed to make comparisons logical and complete.

Comparisons should be made between like items. To compare unlike items is illogical and distracting.

▶ Agnes had an attention span longer than *that of* most of her classmates.

It is illogical to compare an attention span to classmates.

▶ Henry preferred the hotels in Pittsburgh to *those in* Philadelphia.

Hotels must be compared with hotels.

Sometimes the word *other* must be inserted to make a comparison logical.

▶ Chicago is larger than any *other* city in Illinois.

Chicago cannot be larger than itself.

Sometimes the word *as* must be inserted to make a comparison grammatically complete.

▶ Geoffrey is as talented *as*, if not more talented than, the other actors.

The construction *as talented . . . than* is not grammatical.

Comparisons should be complete enough to ensure clarity. Readers should understand what is being compared.

> INCOMPLETE   Brand X is a lighter beer.
>
> COMPLETE   Brand X is a lighter beer than Brand Y.

Also, you should leave no ambiguity about meaning. In the following sentence, two interpretations are possible.

> AMBIGUOUS   Mr. Kelly helped me more than my roommate.
>
> CLEAR   Mr. Kelly helped me more than he helped my roommate.
>
> CLEAR   Mr. Kelly helped me more than my roommate did.

E3

Problems with modifiers

Modifiers, whether they are single words, phrases, or clauses, should point clearly to the words they modify. As a rule, related words should be kept together.

E3-a Put limiting modifiers in front of the words they modify.

Limiting modifiers such as *only, even, almost, nearly,* and *just* should appear in front of a verb only if they modify the verb: *At first I couldn't even touch my toes.* If they limit the meaning of some other word in the sentence, they should be placed in front of that word.

▶ You will ~~only~~ need to plant *only* one package of seeds.

▶ Our team didn't ~~even~~ score *even* once.

E3-b Position phrases and clauses so that readers can see at a glance what they modify.

When whole phrases or clauses are positioned oddly, absurd mis-readings can result.

MISPLACED   The king returned to the clinic where he underwent heart surgery in 1982 in a limousine sent by the White House.

REVISED   Traveling in a limousine sent by the White House, the king returned to the clinic where he underwent heart surgery in 1982.

The king did not undergo heart surgery in a limousine. The revision corrects this false impression.

▶ *On the walls* ~~There~~ are many pictures of comedians who have performed at

Gavin's . ~~on the walls.~~

The comedians weren't performing on the walls; the pictures were on the walls.

► The robber was described as a six-foot-tall man with a mustache *150-pound,* weighing 150 pounds.

The robber, not the mustache, weighed 150 pounds.

E3-c Repair dangling modifiers.

A dangling modifier fails to refer logically to any word in the sentence. Dangling modifiers are usually introductory word groups (such as verbal phrases) that suggest but do not name an actor. When a sentence opens with such a modifier, readers expect the subject of the following clause to name the actor. If it doesn't, the modifier dangles.

DANGLING   Deciding to join the navy, the recruiter enthusiastically pumped Joe's hand. [*participial phrase*]

DANGLING   Upon seeing the barricade, our car screeched to a halt. [*preposition followed by a gerund phrase*]

DANGLING   To please the children, some fireworks were set off a day early. [*infinitive phrase*]

DANGLING   Though only sixteen, UCLA accepted Martha's application. [*elliptical adverb clause with an understood subject and verb*]

These dangling modifiers falsely suggest that the recruiter decided to join the navy, that the car saw the barricade, that the fireworks intended to please the children, and that UCLA is only sixteen years old.

To repair a dangling modifier, you can revise the sentence in one of two ways:

1. Name the actor immediately following the introductory modifier; or
2. turn the modifier into a word group that includes the actor.

► When watching a classic film such as *Gone With the Wind,* *I find* commercials are especially irritating.

▶ When *I am* watching a classic film such as *Gone With the Wind,*

commercials are especially irritating.

A dangling modifier cannot be repaired simply by moving it: *Commercials are especially irritating when watching....* Readers still don't know who is doing the watching.

▶ ~~Opening~~ *When the driver opened* the window to let out a huge bumblebee, the car

accidentally swerved into an oncoming car.

The car didn't open the window; the driver did.

▶ After completing seminary training, ~~women's~~ *women have often been denied* access to the pulpit.

~~has often been denied.~~

The women (not their access to the pulpit) complete seminary training.

E3-d Do not split infinitives needlessly.

When a modifier is inserted between the parts of an infinitive, the result can be awkward. (An infinitive is the word *to* plus a verb.)

▶ ~~The~~ *If possible, the* patient should try to ~~if possible~~ avoid going up and down

stairs.

Usage varies when a split infinitive is less awkward than the preceding one. To be on the safe side, however, you should not split infinitives, especially in formal writing.

▶ The candidate decided to ~~formally~~ launch her campaign. *formally.*

When a split infinitive is more natural and less awkward than alternative phrasing, most readers find it acceptable: *We decided to actually enforce the law* is a perfectly natural construction in English. *We decided actually to enforce the law* is not.

E4

Shifts

Avoid confusing shifts in point of view or in verb tense, mood, or voice.

E4-a Make the point of view consistent in person and number.

The point of view of a piece of writing is the perspective from which it is written: first-person singular (*I*), first-person plural (*we*), second-person singular or plural (*you*), third-person singular (*he, she, it, one*), or third-person plural (*they*). Writers who are having difficulty settling on an appropriate point of view sometimes shift confusingly from one to another. The solution is to choose a suitable perspective and then stay with it.

▶ One week our class met in a junkyard to practice rescuing a

victim trapped in a wrecked car. We learned to dismantle the car

with the essential tools. ~~You~~ *We* were graded on ~~your~~ *our* speed and ~~your~~ *our*

skill in extricating the victim.

The writer should have stayed with the *we* point of view. *You* is inappropriate because the writer is not addressing the reader directly. *You* should not be used in a vague sense meaning *anyone*. (See G3-b.)

▶ ~~Everyone~~ *You* should purchase a lift ticket unless you plan to spend

most of your time walking or crawling up a steep hill.

Here *you* is an appropriate choice, since the writer is giving advice directly to readers.

Shifts from the third-person singular to the third-person plural are especially common.

▶ *Police officers are*
  ~~A police officer is~~ often criticized for always being there when they
     ʌ
aren't needed and never being there when they are.

Although the writer might have changed *they* to *he or she* (to match the singular *officer*), the revision above is more concise. (See also G3-a.)

E4-b Maintain consistent verb tenses.

Consistent verb tenses clearly establish the time of the actions being described. When a passage begins in one tense and then shifts without warning and for no reason to another, readers are distracted and confused.

▶ My hopes ~~rise~~ and ~~fall~~ as Joseph's heart started and stopped. The
           rose   *fell*
   inserted ʌ   *flowed*
doctors ~~insert~~ a large tube into his chest, and blood ~~flows~~ from the
        ʌ   ʌ
incision onto the floor. The tube drained some blood from his lung,

but it was all in vain. At 8:35 P.M. Joseph was declared dead.

Writers often shift verb tenses when writing about literature. The literary convention is to describe fictional events consistently in the present tense. (See G2-c.)

▶ The scarlet letter is a punishment sternly placed on Hester's
                                                    is
breast by the community, and yet it ~~was~~ an extremely fanciful and
                                     ʌ
imaginative product of Hester's own needlework.

E4-c Make verbs consistent in mood and voice.

Unnecessary shifts in the mood of a verb can be as distracting as needless shifts in tense. There are three moods in English: the indicative, used for facts, opinions, and questions; the imperative, used for orders or advice; and the subjunctive, used for wishes or conditions contrary to fact (see G2-d).

The following passage shifts confusingly from the indicative to the imperative mood.

▶ The officers advised against allowing access to our homes without
proper identification. ~~Also~~ alert neighbors to vacation schedules.

They also suggested that we (inserted above) ∧

Since the writer's purpose was to report the officers' advice, the revision puts both sentences in the indicative.

The voice of a verb may be either active (with the subject doing the action) or passive (with the subject receiving the action). (See G2-e.) If a writer shifts without warning from one to the other, readers may be left wondering why.

▶ When the tickets are ready, the travel agent notifies the client/, *lists*

E̶ach ticket ~~is then listed~~ on a daily register form, and a copy of

files

the itinerary . ~~is filed.~~ ∧

The passage began in the active voice (*agent notifies*) and then switched to the passive (*ticket is listed . . . copy is filed*). Because the active voice is clearer and more direct, the revision puts the verbs consistently in the active voice.

E5

Mixed constructions

A mixed construction contains parts that do not sensibly fit together. The mismatch may be a matter of grammar or of logic.

E5-a Untangle the grammatical structure.

A writer should not begin with one grammatical plan and then switch without warning to another.

▶ ~~For~~ M̶ost drivers who have a blood alcohol content of .05 percent

double their risk of causing an accident.

The prepositional phrase beginning with *For* cannot serve as the subject of a sentence.

▶ Although I feel that Mr. Dawe is an excellent calculus instructor,

~~but~~ a few minor changes in his method would benefit both him

and the class.

The *although* clause is subordinate, so it cannot be linked to an independent clause with the coordinating conjunction *but*.

Occasionally a mixed construction is so tangled that it defies grammatical analysis. When this happens, back away from the sentence, rethink what you want to say, and then say it again as clearly as you can.

MIXED   In the whole-word method children learn to recognize entire words rather than by the phonics method in which they learn to sound out letters and groups of letters.

REVISED   The whole-word method teaches children to recognize entire words; the phonics method teaches them to sound out letters and groups of letters.

E5-b Straighten out the logical connections.

The subject and the predicate should make sense together. When they don't, the error is known as *faulty predication*.

▶ The ~~growth in the~~ number of applications is increasing rapidly.

It is not the growth that is increasing but the number of applications.

▶ Under the revised plan, the ^double personal exemption for the elderly, ~~who now receive a double~~

~~personal exemption,~~ will be abolished.

The exemption, not the elderly, will be abolished.

E5-c Avoid . . . *is when,* . . . *is where,* and *reason . . . is because* constructions.

In formal English many readers object to . . . *is when,* . . . *is where,* and *reason . . . is because* constructions on either logical or grammatical grounds.

▶ Anorexia nervosa is ~~where people,~~ believing they are too fat, diet

a disorder suffered by people who,

to the point of starvation.

Anorexia nervosa is a disorder, not a place.

▶ ~~The reason~~ I missed the exam ~~is~~ because my motorcycle broke

down.

A *because* clause is adverbial; therefore, it cannot serve as the subject complement of the linking verb *is*. The writer might have replaced the word *because* with *that,* but the revision above is more concise.

E6

Coordination and subordination

When combining ideas in one sentence, use coordination to create equal emphasis and use subordination to create unequal emphasis.

Coordination

Coordination draws equal attention to two or more ideas. To coordinate words or phrases, join them with a coordinating conjunction (*and, but, or, nor, for, so, yet*). To coordinate independent clauses (word groups that can stand alone as sentences), join them with a comma and a coordinating conjunction or with a semicolon. The semicolon is often accompanied by a conjunctive adverb such as *therefore, moreover,* or *however.*

Grandmother lost her sight, but her hearing sharpened.

Grandmother lost her sight; however, her hearing sharpened.

Subordination

To give unequal emphasis to two or more ideas, express the major idea in an independent clause and place any minor ideas in phrases or subordinate clauses. (See R3-e.) Subordinate clauses, which cannot stand alone, typically begin with one of the following words.

after	before	unless	whether	whom
although	if	until	which	whose
as	since	when	while	
because	that	where	who	

Deciding which idea to emphasize is not simply a matter of right and wrong. Consider the two ideas mentioned earlier.

Grandmother lost her sight. Her hearing sharpened.

If your purpose is to stress your grandmother's acute hearing rather than her blindness, subordinate the idea concerning her blindness.

As Grandmother lost her sight, her hearing sharpened.

To focus on your grandmother's blindness, subordinate the idea concerning her hearing.

Though her hearing sharpened, Grandmother gradually lost her sight.

E6-a Combine choppy sentences.

Short sentences demand attention, so they should be used primarily for emphasis. Too many short sentences, one after the other, create a choppy style.

If an idea is not important enough to deserve its own sentence, try combining it with a sentence close by. Put any minor ideas in subordinate structures such as phrases or subordinate clauses.

CHOPPY   The huts vary in height. They measure from ten to fifteen feet in diameter. They contain no modern conveniences.

IMPROVED The huts, which vary in height and measure from ten to fifteen feet in diameter, contain no modern conveniences.

Three sentences have become one, with minor ideas expressed in a subordinate clause beginning with *which*.

▶ Agnes , ~~was~~ another student I worked with /, ~~She~~ was a hyperactive child.

A minor idea is now expressed in an appositive phrase describing Agnes.

▶ *Although the* ~~The~~ Market Inn, ~~is~~ located at 2nd and E streets, ~~It~~ doesn't look very impressive from the outside, ~~The~~ food, ~~however,~~ is excellent.

Minor ideas are now expressed in a subordinate clause (*Although . . . outside*) and a phrase (*located . . . streets*).

Although subordination is ordinarily the most effective technique for combining short, choppy sentences, coordination is appropriate when the ideas are equal in importance.

▶ The hospital decides when patients will sleep and wake, ~~It~~ *and* dictates what and when they will eat, ~~It~~ tells them when they may be with family and friends.

Three sentences have become one, with equivalent ideas expressed in a coordinate series.

E6-b Avoid ineffective coordination.

Coordinate structures are appropriate only when you intend to draw the reader's attention equally to two or more ideas: *Schwegler praises loudly, and he criticizes softly.* If one idea is more important than another — or if a coordinating conjunction does not clearly signal the relation between the ideas — the lesser idea should be subordinated.

INEFFECTIVE   Closets were taxed as rooms, and most colonists stored their clothes in chests or clothes presses.

IMPROVED   Because closets were taxed as rooms, most colonists stored their clothes in chests or clothes presses.

The revision puts the less important idea in a subordinate clause beginning with *Because*. Notice that the subordinating conjunction *because* signals the relation between the ideas more clearly than the coordinating conjunction *and*.

▶ My uncle, *noticing* ~~noticed~~ the frightened look on my face, ~~and~~ told me

that Grandma had to feel my face because she was blind.

The less important idea has become a participial phrase modifying the noun *uncle*.

▶ *After four hours,* ~~Four hours went by, and~~ a rescue truck finally arrived, but by

that time we had been evacuated in a helicopter.

Three independent clauses were excessive. The least important idea has become a prepositional phrase.

E6-c Do not subordinate major ideas.

If a sentence buries its major idea in a subordinate construction, readers are not likely to give it enough attention. Express the major idea in an independent clause and subordinate any minor ideas.

▶ *As* I was driving home from my new job, heading down New York

Avenue, ~~when~~ my car suddenly overheated.

The revision puts the major idea—that the car overheated—in the independent clause and subordinates the other information.

E6-d Do not subordinate excessively.

In attempting to avoid short, choppy sentences, writers sometimes move to the opposite extreme, putting more subordinate ideas into a sentence than readers can easily handle.

▶ Our job is to stay between the stacker and the tie machine

watching to see if the newspapers jam, *If they do,* ~~in which case~~ we pull the

bundles off and stack them on a skid, because otherwise they

would back up in the stacker and the press would have to be

turned off.

E7

Sentence variety

When a rough draft is filled with too many same-sounding sentences, try to inject some variety — as long as you can do so without sacrificing clarity or ease of reading.

E7-a Use a variety of sentence structures.

A writer should not rely too heavily on simple sentences and compound sentences, for the effect tends to be both monotonous and choppy. (See E6-a and E6-b.) Too many complex or compound-complex sentences, however, can be equally monotonous. If your style tends to one or the other extreme, try to achieve a better mix of sentence types.

For a discussion of sentence types, see R4.

E7-b Use a variety of sentence openings.

Most sentences in English begin with the subject, move to the verb, and continue to an object, with modifiers tucked in along the way or put at the end. For the most part, such sentences are fine. Put too many of them in a row, however, and they become monotonous.

Adverbial modifiers can often be inserted ahead of the subject. Such modifiers might be single words, phrases, or clauses.

▶ *Eventually a* A few drops of sap ~~eventually~~ began to trickle into the pail.

▶ *Just as the sun was coming up, a* A pair of black ducks flew over the blind. ~~just as the sun was coming up.~~

Adjectives and participial phrases can frequently be moved to the beginning of a sentence without loss of clarity.

▶ *Dejected and withdrawn,* Edward, ~~dejected and withdrawn,~~ nearly gave up his search for a job.

▶ ~~John and I,~~ anticipating a peaceful evening, sat down at the

A   *John and I*

campfire to brew a cup of coffee.

CAUTION: When beginning a sentence with an adjective or a participial phrase, make sure that the subject of the sentence names the person or thing described in the introductory phrase. If it doesn't, the phrase will dangle. (See E3-c.)

E7-c Try inverting sentences occasionally.

A sentence is inverted if it does not follow the normal subject-verb-object pattern. Many inversions sound artificial and should be avoided except in the most formal contexts. But if an inversion sounds natural, it can provide a welcome touch of variety.

Opposite the produce section is a

▶ ~~A~~ refrigerated case of mouth-watering cheeses. ~~is opposite the~~

~~produce section.~~

Set at the top two corners of the stage were huge

▶ ~~Huge~~ lavender hearts outlined in bright white lights. ~~were set at~~

~~the top two corners of the stage.~~

Word Choice

W

Word Choice

W1

Glossary of usage

This glossary includes words commonly confused (such as *accept* and *except*), words commonly misused (such as *hopefully*), and words that are nonstandard (such as *hisself*). It also lists colloquialisms and jargon. Colloquialisms are expressions that may be appropriate in informal speech but are inappropriate in formal writing. Jargon is needlessly technical or pretentious language that is inappropriate in most contexts.

a, an Use *an* before a vowel sound, *a* before a consonant sound: *an apple, a peach.* Problems sometimes arise with words beginning with *h.* If the *h* is silent, the word begins with a vowel sound, so use *an*: *an hour, an heir, an honest senator, an honorable deed.* If the *h* is pronounced, the word begins with a consonant sound, so use *a*: *a hospital, a hymn, a historian, a hotel.*

accept, except *Accept* is a verb meaning "to receive." *Except* is usually a preposition meaning "excluding." *I will accept all the packages except that one. Except* is also a verb meaning "to exclude." *Please except that item from the list.*

adapt, adopt *Adapt* means "to adjust or become accustomed"; it is usually followed by *to. Adopt* means "to take as one's own." *Our family adopted a Vietnamese orphan, who quickly adapted to his new surroundings.*

adverse, averse *Adverse* means "unfavorable." *Averse* means "opposed" or "reluctant"; it is usually followed by "to." *I am averse to your proposal because it could have an adverse impact on the economy.*

advice, advise *Advice* is a noun, *advise* a verb: *We advise you to follow John's advice.*

affect, effect *Affect* is usually a verb meaning "to influence." *Effect* is usually a noun meaning "result." *The drug did not affect the disease, and it had several adverse side effects. Effect* can also be a verb meaning "to bring about." *Only the president can effect such a dramatic change.*

aggravate *Aggravate* means "to make worse or more troublesome": *Overgrazing aggravated the soil erosion.* In formal writing, avoid the colloquial use of *aggravate* meaning "to annoy or irritate." *Her babbling annoyed* (not *aggravated*) *me.*

agree to, agree with *Agree to* means "to give consent." *Agree with* means "to be in accord" or "to come to an understanding." *He agrees with me about the need for change, but he won't agree to my plan.*

ain't *Ain't* is nonstandard. Use *am not, are not (aren't),* or *is not (isn't). I am not* (not *ain't*) *going home for spring break.*

all ready, already *All ready* means "completely prepared." *Already* means "previously." *Susan was all ready for the concert, but her friends had already left.*

all right *All right* is always written as two words. *Alright* is nonstandard.

all together, altogether *All together* means "everyone gathered." *Altogether* means "entirely." *We were not altogether certain that we could bring the family all together for the reunion.*

allude To *allude* to something is to make an indirect reference to it. Do not use *allude* to mean "to refer directly." *In his lecture the professor referred* (not *alluded*) *to several pre-Socratic philosophers.*

allusion, illusion An *allusion* is an indirect reference. An *illusion* is a misconception or false impression. *Did you catch my allusion to Shakespeare? Mirrors give the room an illusion of depth.*

a lot *A lot* is two words. Do not write *alot. We have had a lot of rain this spring.* See also *lots, lots of.*

A.M., P.M., a.m., p.m. Use these abbreviations with numerals: *6 P.M., 11 a.m.* Do not use them as substitutes for the words *morning* and *evening. I worked until late in the evening* (not *p.m.*) *yesterday.*

among, between Ordinarily, use *among* with three or more entities, *between* with two. *The prize was divided among several contestants. You have a choice between carrots and beans.*

amoral, immoral *Amoral* means "neither moral nor immoral"; it also means "not caring about moral judgments." *Immoral* means "morally wrong." *Until recently, most business courses were taught from an amoral perspective. Murder is immoral.*

amount, number Use *amount* with quantities that cannot be counted; use *number* with those that can. *This recipe calls for a large amount of sugar. We have a large number of toads in our garden.*

an See *a, an.*

and etc. *Et cetera (etc.)* means "and so forth"; therefore, *and etc.* is redundant. See also *etc.*

and/or Avoid the awkward construction *and/or* except in technical or legal documents.

angry at, angry with To write that one is *angry at* another person is nonstandard. Use *angry with* instead.

ante-, anti- The prefix *ante-* means "earlier" or "in front of"; the prefix *anti-* means "against" or "opposed to." *William Lloyd Garrison was one of the leaders of the antislavery movement during the antebellum period.*

Anti- should be used with a hyphen when it is followed by a capital letter or a word beginning with *i*.

anxious *Anxious* means "worried" or "apprehensive." In formal writing, avoid using *anxious* to mean "eager": *We are eager* (not *anxious*) *to see your new house.*

anybody *Anybody* is singular. (See G1-d and G3-a.)

anymore Reserve the adverb *anymore* for negative contexts, where it means "any longer." *Moviegoers are rarely shocked anymore by profanity.* Do not use *anymore* in positive contexts. Use *now* or *nowadays* instead. *Interest rates are so high nowadays* (not *anymore*) *that few people can afford to buy homes.*

anyone *Anyone* is singular. (See G1-d and G3-a.)

anyone, any one *Anyone,* an indefinite pronoun, means "any person at all." *Any one,* the pronoun *one* preceded by the adjective *any,* refers to a particular person or thing in a group. *Anyone from Chicago may choose any one of the games on display.*

anyplace *Anyplace* is informal for *anywhere.*

anyways, anywheres *Anyways* and *anywheres* are nonstandard for *anyway* and *anywhere.*

as *As* is sometimes used to mean "because." But do not use it if there is any chance of ambiguity: *We canceled the picnic because* (not *as*) *it began raining.* An *as* here could mean "because" or "when."

as, like See *like, as.*

averse See *adverse, averse.*

awful The adjective *awful* means "awe-inspiring." Colloquially it is used to mean "terrible" or "bad." The adverb *awfully* is sometimes used in conversation as an intensifier meaning "very." In formal writing, avoid these colloquial uses. *I was very* (not *awfully*) *upset last night.*

awhile, a while *Awhile* is an adverb; it can modify a verb, but it cannot be the object of a preposition such as *for.* The two-word form *a while* is a noun preceded by an article and therefore can be the object of a preposition. *Stay awhile. Stay for a while.*

bad, badly *Bad* is an adjective, *badly* an adverb. (See G4.) *They felt bad about being early and ruining the surprise. Her arm hurt badly after she slid headfirst into second base.*

being as, being that *Being as* and *being that* are nonstandard expressions. Write *because* or *since* instead. *Because* (not *being as*) *I slept late, I had to skip breakfast.*

beside, besides *Beside* is a preposition meaning "at the side of" or "next to." *Annie Oakley slept with her gun beside her bed. Besides* is a preposition meaning "except" or "in addition to." *No one besides Terrie can* *have that ice cream. Besides* is also an adverb meaning "in addition." *I'm not hungry; besides, I don't like ice cream.*

between See *among, between.*

bring, take Use *bring* when an object is being transported toward you, *take* when it is being moved away. *Please bring me a glass of water. Please take these flowers to Mr. Scott.*

burst, bursted; bust, busted *Burst* is an irregular verb meaning "to come open or fly apart suddenly or violently." Its principal parts are *burst, burst, burst.* The past-tense form *bursted* is nonstandard. *Bust* and *busted* are slang for *burst* and, along with *bursted,* should not be used in formal writing.

can, may The distinction between *can* and *may* is fading, but many careful writers still observe it in formal writing. *Can* is traditionally reserved for ability, *may* for permission. *Can you ski down the advanced slope without falling? May I help you?*

capital, capitol *Capital* refers to a city, *capitol* to a building where lawmakers meet. *Capital* also refers to wealth or resources. *The capitol has undergone extensive renovations. The residents of the state capital protested the development plans.*

censor, censure *Censor* means "to remove or suppress material considered objectionable." Censure means "to criticize severely." *The library's new policy of censoring controversial books has been censured by the media.*

center around *Center on* and *center in* are considered more logical than *center around. His talk centered on the global buildup of arms in the last five years.*

cite, site *Cite* means "to quote as an authority or example." *Site,* as a verb, means "to situate or locate." *He cited* (not *sited*) *Frank Lloyd Wright to give strength to his argument.*

climactic, climatic *Climactic* is derived from *climax,* the point of greatest intensity in a series or progression of events. *Climatic* is derived from *climate* and refers to meteorological conditions. *The climactic period in the dinosaurs' reign was reached just before severe climatic conditions brought on an ice age.*

compare to, compare with *Compare to* means "to represent as similar." *She compared him to a wild stallion. Compare with* means "to examine the ways in which two things are similar." *The study compared the language ability of apes with that of dolphins.*

complement, compliment *Complement* is a verb meaning "to go with or complete" or a noun meaning "something that completes." *Compliment* as a verb means "to flatter"; as a noun it means "flattering remark." *Her skill at rushing the net complements his skill at volleying. Mother's flower arrangements receive many compliments.*

conscience, conscious *Conscience* is a noun meaning "moral principles." *Conscious* is an adjective meaning "aware or alert." *Let your conscience be your guide. Were you conscious of his love for you?*

contact Although the use of *contact* to mean "to get in touch with" is common in speech, it is not appropriate in formal writing. If possible, use a precise verb such as *write* or *telephone*. *We will telephone* (not *contact*) *you soon.*

continual, continuous *Continual* means "repeated regularly and frequently." *She grew weary of the continual telephone calls. Continuous* means "extended or prolonged without interruption." *The broken siren made a continuous wail.*

could care less *Could care less* is a nonstandard expression. Write *couldn't care less* instead. *He couldn't* (not *could*) *care less about his psychology final.*

could of *Could of* is nonstandard for *could have. We could have* (not *could of*) *had steak for dinner if we had been hungry.*

criteria *Criteria* is the plural of *criterion,* which means "a standard, or rule, or test on which a judgment or decision can be based." *The only criterion for the scholarship is ability.*

data *Data* is the plural of *datum,* which means "a fact or proposition." Many writers now treat *data* as singular or plural depending on the meaning of the sentence. Some experts insist, however, that *data* can only be plural. *The new data suggest* (not *suggests*) *that our theory is correct.* The singular form *datum* is rarely used.

deal *Deal* is a colloquial expression for "bargain," "business transaction," or "agreement." *We made a deal.* Avoid such colloquial use in formal writing.

different from, different than Ordinarily, write *different from. Your sense of style is different from Jim's.* However, *different than* is acceptable to avoid an awkward construction. *Please let me know if your plans are different than* (to avoid *from what*) *they were six weeks ago.*

differ from, differ with *Differ from* means "to be unlike"; *differ with* means "to disagree." *She differed with me about the wording of the agreement. My approach to the problem differed from hers.*

disinterested, uninterested *Disinterested* means "impartial, objective"; *uninterested* means "not interested." *We sought the advice of a disinterested counselor to help us solve our problem. He was uninterested in anyone's opinion but his own.*

don't *Don't* is the contraction for *do not. I don't want any. Don't* should not be used as the contraction for *does not,* which is *doesn't. He doesn't* (not *don't*) *want any.* (See also G1.)

double negative Standard English allows two negatives only if a positive meaning is intended. *The runners were not unhappy with their performance.* Double negatives used to emphasize negation are nonstandard. *Jack doesn't have to answer to anybody* (not *nobody*).

due to   *Due to* is an adjective phrase and should not be used as a preposition meaning "because of." *The trip was canceled because of* (not *due to*) *lack of interest. Due to* is acceptable as a subject complement and usually follows a form of the verb *be. His success was due to hard work.*

each   *Each* is singular. (See G1-d and G3-a.)

effect   See *affect, effect.*

e.g.   In formal writing, replace the Latin abbreviation *e.g.* with its English equivalent: *for example* or *for instance.*

either   *Either* is singular. (See G1-d and G3-a.) For *either . . . or* constructions, see G1-c.

elicit, illicit   *Elicit* is a verb meaning "to bring out" or "to evoke." *Illicit* is an adjective meaning "unlawful." *The reporter was unable to elicit any information from the police about illicit drug traffic.*

emigrate from, immigrate to   *Emigrate* means "to leave one country or region to settle in another." *In 1900, my grandfather emigrated from Russia to escape the religious pogroms. Immigrate* means "to enter another country and reside there." *Many Mexicans immigrate to the United States to find work.*

eminent, imminent   *Eminent* means "outstanding" or "distinguished." *We met an eminent professor of Greek history. Imminent* means "about to happen." *The announcement is imminent.*

enthused   Many people object to the use of *enthused* as an adjective. Use *enthusiastic* instead. *The children were enthusiastic* (not *enthused*) *about going to the circus.*

-ess   Many people find the *-ess* suffix demeaning. Write *poet,* not *poetess; Jew,* not *Jewess; author,* not *authoress.*

etc.   Avoid ending a list with *etc.* It is more emphatic to end with an example, and in most contexts readers will understand that the list is not exhaustive. When you don't wish to end with an example, *and so on* is more graceful than *etc.* See also *and etc.*

eventually, ultimately   Although these words are often used interchangeably, *eventually* is the better choice to mean "at an unspecified time in the future" and *ultimately* is better to mean "the furthest possible extent or greatest extreme." *He knew that eventually he would complete his degree. The existentialist considered suicide the ultimately rational act.*

everybody, everyone   *Everybody* and *everyone* are singular. (See G1-d and G3-a.)

everyone, every one *Everyone* is an indefinite pronoun. *Every one,* the pronoun *one* preceded by the adjective *every,* means "each individual or thing in a particular group." *Every one* is usually followed by *of. Everyone wanted to go. Every one of the missing books was found.*

exam *Exam* is informal for *examination.*

except See *accept, except.*

expect Avoid the colloquial use of *expect* meaning "to believe, think, or suppose." *I think* (not *expect*) *it will rain tonight.*

explicit, implicit *Explicit* means "expressed directly" or "clearly defined"; *implicit* means "implied, unstated." *I gave him explicit instructions not to go swimming. My mother's silence indicated her implicit approval.*

farther, further *Farther* describes distances. *Chicago is farther from Miami than I thought. Further* suggests quantity or degree. *You extended the curfew further than you should have.*

female, male The terms *female* and *male* are jargon for "woman" and "man." *Two women* (not *females*) *and one man* (not *male*) *applied for the position.*

fewer, less *Fewer* refers to items that can be counted; *less* refers to general amounts. *Fewer people are living in the city, so real estate is less expensive.*

finalize *Finalize* is jargon meaning "to make final or complete." Use ordinary English instead.

firstly *Firstly* sounds pretentious, and it leads to the ungainly series *firstly, secondly, thirdly, fourthly,* and so on. Write *first, second, third* instead.

flunk *Flunk* is colloquial for *fail* and should be avoided in formal writing.

folks *Folks* is an informal expression for "parents" or "relatives" or "people" in general. Use a more formal expression instead.

further See *farther, further.*

get *Get* has many colloquial uses. In writing, avoid using *get* to mean the following: "to evoke an emotional response" (*That music always gets to me*); "to annoy" (*After a while his sulking got to me*); "to take revenge on" (*I got back at him by leaving the room*); "to become" (*He got sick*); "to start or begin" (*Let's get going*). Avoid using *have got to* in place of *must. I must* (not *have got to*) *finish this paper tonight.*

good, well *Good* is an adjective, *well* an adverb. See G4. *He hasn't felt good about his game since he sprained his wrist last season. She performed well on the uneven parallel bars.*

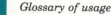

hanged, hung *Hanged* is the past-tense and past-participle form of the verb *hang* meaning "to execute." *The prisoner was hanged at dawn.* *Hung* is the past-tense and past-participle form of the verb *hang* meaning "to fasten or suspend." *The stockings were hung by the chimney with care.*

hardly Avoid expressions such as *can't hardly* and *not hardly*, which are considered double negatives. *I can* (not *can't*) *hardly describe my elation at getting the job.*

has got, have got *Got* is unnecessary and awkward in such constructions. It should be dropped. *We have* (not *have got*) *three days to prepare for the opening.*

he At one time it was acceptable to use *he* to mean "he or she." Today such usage is inappropriate. See G3-a and W3-e for alternative constructions.

he/she, his/her In formal writing, use *he or she* or *his or her*. For alternatives to these wordy constructions, see G3-a and W3-e.

hisself *Hisself* is nonstandard. Use *himself*.

hopefully *Hopefully* means "in a hopeful manner." *We looked hopefully to the future.* Do not use *hopefully* in constructions such as the following: *Hopefully, your daughter will recover soon.* Indicate who is doing the hoping: *I hope that your daughter will recover soon.*

hung See *hanged, hung*.

i.e. In formal writing, replace the Latin abbreviation *i.e.* with its English equivalent: *that is*.

if, whether Use *if* in a statement of condition and *whether* to express alternatives. *If you go on a trip, whether it be to Nebraska or New Jersey, remember to bring traveler's checks.*

illusion See *allusion, illusion*.

imminent See *eminent, imminent*.

immoral See *amoral, immoral*.

implement *Implement* is a pretentious way of saying "do," "carry out," or "accomplish." Use ordinary language instead. *We carried out* (not *implemented*) *the director's orders with some reluctance.*

imply, infer *Imply* means "to suggest or state indirectly"; *infer* means "to draw a conclusion." *John implied that he knew all about computers, but the interviewer inferred that John was inexperienced.*

in, into *In* indicates location or condition; *into* indicates movement or a change in condition. *They found the lost letters in a box after moving into the house.*

individual *Individual* is a pretentious substitute for *person*. *We invited* *several persons* (not *individuals*) *from the audience to participate in the experiment.*

ingenious, ingenuous   *Ingenious* means "clever." *Sarah's solution to the problem was ingenious. Ingenuous* means "naive" or "frank." *For a successful manager, Ed is surprisingly ingenuous.*

in regards to   *In regards to* confuses two different phrases: *in regard to* and *as regards.* Use one or the other. *In regard to* (or *as regards*) *the contract, ignore the first clause.*

irregardless   *Irregardless* is nonstandard. Use *regardless.*

is when, is where   These mixed constructions are often incorrectly used in definitions. *A run-off election is a second election held to break a tie* (not *is when a second election breaks a tie*). (See E5-c.)

its, it's   *Its* is a possessive pronoun; *it's* is a contraction for *it is.* (See P5-e.) *The dog licked its wound whenever its owner walked into the room. It's a perfect day to walk the twenty-mile trail.*

kind(s)   *Kind* is singular and should be treated as such. Don't write *These kind of chairs are rare.* Write instead *This kind of chair is rare. Kinds* is plural and should be used only when you mean more than one kind. *These kinds of chairs are rare.*

kind of, sort of   Avoid using *kind of* or *sort of* to mean "somewhat." *The movie was kind of boring.* Do not put *a* after either phrase. *That kind of* (not *kind of a*) *salesclerk annoys me.*

learn, teach   *Learn* means "to gain knowledge"; *teach* means "to impart knowledge." *I must teach* (not *learn*) *my sister to read.*

leave, let   Avoid the nonstandard use of *leave* ("to exit") to mean *let* ("to permit"). *Let* (not *leave*) *me help you with the dishes.*

less   See *fewer, less.*

let, leave   See *leave, let.*

liable   *Liable* means "obligated" or "responsible." Do not use it to mean "likely." *You're likely* (not *liable*) *to trip if you don't tie your shoelaces.*

lie, lay   *Lie* is an intransitive verb meaning "to recline or rest on a surface." Its principal parts are *lie, lay, lain. Lay* is a transitive verb meaning "to put or place." Its principal parts are *lay, laid, laid.* (See G2-b.)

like, as   *Like* is a preposition, not a subordinating conjunction. It is followed only by a noun or a noun phrase. *As* is a subordinating conjunction that introduces a subordinate clause. In casual speech you may say *She looks like she hasn't slept* or *You don't know her like I do.* But in formal writing, use *as. She looks as if she hasn't slept. You don't know her as I do.* See prepositions and subordinating conjunctions, R3-a and R3-e.

loan   Some people object to the use of *loan* as a verb. Use *lend* instead. *Please lend* (not *loan*) *me five dollars.*

loose, lose   *Loose* is an adjective meaning "not securely fastened." *Lose* is a verb meaning "to misplace" or "to not win." *Did you lose your only loose pair of work pants?*

lots, lots of   *Lots* and *lots of* are colloquial substitutes for *many, much,* or *a lot*. Avoid using them in formal writing.

male, female   See *female, male.*

mankind   Avoid *mankind* whenever possible. It offends many readers because it excludes women. Use *humanity, humans, the human race,* or *humankind* instead.

may   See *can, may.*

maybe, may be   *Maybe* is an adverb meaning "possibly." *May be* is a verb phrase. *Maybe the sun will shine tomorrow. Tomorrow may be a brighter day.*

may of, might of   *May of* and *might of* are nonstandard for *may have* and *might have. We may have* (not *may of*) *had too many cookies.*

media, medium   *Media* is the plural of *medium. Of all the media that cover the Olympics, television is the medium that best captures the spectacle of the events.*

most   *Most* is colloquial when used to mean "almost" and should be avoided. *Almost* (not *most*) *everyone went to the parade.*

must of   See *may of.*

myself   *Myself* is a reflexive or intensive pronoun. Reflexive: *I cut myself.* Intensive: *I will drive you myself.* Do not use *myself* in place of *I* or *me. He gave the flowers to Melinda and me* (not *myself*). (See also G3-c.)

nauseated, nauseous   *Nauseated* means "suffering from nausea." *Nauseous* means "causing nausea." *I feel nauseated* (not *nauseous*).

neither   *Neither* is singular. See G1-d and G3-a. For *neither . . . nor* constructions, see G1-c.

none   *None* is singular. (See G1-d and G3-a.)

nowheres   *Nowheres* is nonstandard for *nowhere.*

number   See *amount, number.*

of   Use the verb *have,* not the preposition *of,* after the verbs *could, should, would, may, might,* and *must. They must have* (not *of*) *left early.*

off of   *Off* is sufficient. Omit *of. The ball rolled off* (not *off of*) *the table.*

OK, O.K., okay   All three spellings are acceptable, but in formal speech and writing avoid these colloquial expressions for consent or approval.

parameters *Parameter* is a mathematical term that has become jargon for "fixed limit," "boundary," or "guideline." Use ordinary English instead. *The task force was asked to work within certain guidelines* (not *parameters*).

percent, per cent, percentage *Percent* (also spelled *per cent*) is always used with a specific number. *Percentage* is used with a descriptive term such as *large* or *small,* not with a specific number. *The candidate won 80 percent of the primary vote. Only a small percentage of registered voters turned out for the election.*

phenomena *Phenomena* is the plural of *phenomenon,* which means "an observable occurrence or fact." *Strange phenomena occur at all hours of the night in that house, but last night's phenomenon was the strangest of all.*

plus *Plus* should not be used to join independent clauses. *This raincoat is dirty; moreover* (not *plus*), *it has a hole in it.*

precede, proceed *Precede* means "to come before." *Proceed* means "to go forward." *As we proceeded up the mountain, we noticed fresh tracks in the mud, evidence that a group of hikers had preceded us.*

principal, principle *Principal* is a noun meaning "the head of a school or organization" or "a sum of money." It is also an adjective meaning "most important." *Principle* is a noun meaning "a basic truth or law." *The principal expelled her for three principal reasons. We believe in the principle of equal justice for all.*

proceed, precede See *precede, proceed.*

quote, quotation *Quote* is a verb; *quotation* is a noun. Avoid using *quote* as a shortened form of the noun. *Her quotations* (not *quotes*) *from Shakespeare intrigued us.*

raise, rise *Raise* is a transitive verb meaning "to move or cause to move upward." It takes a direct object. *I raised the shades. Rise* is an intransitive verb meaning "to go up." It does not take a direct object. *Heat rises.*

real, really *Real* is an adjective; *really* is an adverb. *Real* is sometimes used informally as an adverb, but avoid this use in formal writing. *She was really* (not *real*) *angry.* (See G4.)

reason is because Use *that* instead of *because. The reason I'm late is that* (not *because*) *my car broke down.* (See E5-c.)

reason why The expression *reason why* is redundant. *The reason* (not *the reason why*) *Jones lost the election is clear.*

relation, relationship *Relation* describes a connection between things. *There is a relation between poverty and infant mortality. Relationship* describes a connection between people. *Our business relationship has cooled over the years.*

respectfully, respectively   *Respectfully* means "showing or marked by respect." *He respectfully submitted his opinion to the judge. Respectively* means "each in the order given." *John, Tom, and Larry were a butcher, a baker, and a lawyer, respectively.*

sensual, sensuous   *Sensual* means "gratifying the physical senses," especially those associated with sexual pleasure. *Sensuous* means "pleasing to the senses," especially those involved in the experience of art, music, and nature. *The sensuous music and balmy air led the dancers to more sensual movements.*

set, sit   *Set* is a transitive verb meaning "to put" or "to place." Its principal parts are *set, set, set. Sit* is an intransitive verb meaning "to be seated." Its principal parts are *sit, sat, sat. She set the dough in a warm corner of the kitchen. The cat sat in the warmest part of the room, directly over the furnace.*

shall, will   *Shall* was once used as the helping verb with *I* or *we*: *I shall, we shall, you will, he/she/it will, they will.* Today, however, *will* is generally accepted even when the subject is *I* or *we*. The word *shall* occurs primarily in polite questions (*Shall I find you a pillow?*) and in legalistic sentences suggesting duty or obligation (*The applicant shall file form 1080 by December 31*).

should of   *Should of* is nonstandard for *should have. They should have* (not *should of*) *been home an hour ago.*

since   Do not use *since* to mean *because* if there is any chance of ambiguity. *Since we won the game, we have been celebrating with a pitcher of beer. Since* here could mean "because" or "from the time that."

sit   See *set, sit.*

site, cite   See *cite, site.*

somebody, someone   *Somebody* and *someone* are singular. (See G1-d and G3-a.)

something   *Something* is singular. (See G1-d and G3-a.)

sometime, some time, sometimes   *Sometime* is an adverb meaning "at an indefinite or unstated time." *I'll see you sometime soon. Some time* is the adjective *some* modifying the noun *time* and is spelled as two words to mean "a period of time." *I haven't lived there for some time. Sometimes* is an adverb meaning "at times, now and then." *Sometimes I run into him at the library.*

sure and   *Sure and* is nonstandard for *sure to. We were all taught to be sure to* (not *and*) *look both ways before crossing a street.*

take   See *bring, take.*

than, then   *Than* is a conjunction used in comparisons; *then* is an adverb denoting time. *That pizza is more than I can eat. Tom laughed, and then we recognized him.*

that See *who, which, that.*

that, which Many writers reserve *that* for restrictive clauses, *which* for nonrestrictive clauses. (See P1-e.)

theirselves *Theirselves* is nonstandard for *themselves. The two people were able to push the Volkswagen out of the way themselves* (not *theirselves*).

there, their, they're *There* is an adverb specifying place; it is also an expletive. Adverb: *Sylvia is lying there unconscious.* Expletive: *There are two plums left. Their* is a possessive pronoun: *Fred and Jane finally washed their car. They're* is a contraction of *they are: They're later than usual today.*

this kind See *kind(s).*

to, too, two *To* is a preposition; *too* is an adverb; *two* is a number. *Too many of your shots slice to the left, but the last two were right on the mark.*

toward, towards *Toward* an *towards* are generally interchangeable, although *toward* is preferred.

try and *Try and* is nonstandard for *try to. The teacher asked us all to try to* (not *and*) *write an original haiku.*

ultimately, eventually See *eventually, ultimately.*

unique Avoid expressions such as *most unique, more straight, less perfect, very round.* Something either is unique or it isn't. It is illogical to suggest degrees of uniqueness. (See G4-c.)

usage The noun *usage* should not be substituted for *use* when the meaning intended is "employment of." *The use* (not *usage*) *of computers dramatically increased the company's profits.*

use to, suppose to *Use to* and *suppose to* are nonstandard for *used to* and *supposed to.*

utilize *utilize* means "to make use of." It often sounds pretentious; in most cases, *use* is sufficient. *I used* (not *utilized*) *the best workers to get the job done fast.*

wait for, wait on *Wait for* means "to be in readiness for" or "await." *Wait on* means "to serve." *We're only waiting for* (not *waiting on*) *Ruth before we can leave.*

ways *Ways* is colloquial when used to mean "distance." *The city is a long way* (not *ways*) *from here.*

where Do not use *where* in place of *that. I heard that* (not *where*) *the crime rate is increasing.*

which   See *that, which* and *who, which, that.*

while   Avoid using *while* to mean "although" or "whereas" if there is any chance of ambiguity. *Although* (not *While*) *Gloria lost money in the slot machine, Tom won it at roulette.* Here *while* could mean either "although" or "at the same time that."

who, which, that   Do not use *which* to refer to persons. Use *who* instead. *That,* though generally used to refer to things, may be used to refer to a group or class of people. *Fans wondered how an old man who* (not *that* or *which*) *walked with a limp could play football. The team that scores the most points in this game will win the tournament.*

who, whom   *Who* is used for subjects and subject complements; *whom* is used for objects. (See G3-d.)

who's, whose   *Who's* is a contraction of *who is; whose* is a possessive pronoun. *Who's ready for more popcorn? Whose coat is this?*

will   See *shall, will.*

would of   *Would of* is nonstandard for *would have. She would have* (not *would of*) *had a chance to play if she had arrived on time.*

you   In formal writing, avoid *you* in an indefinite sense meaning "anyone." See G3-b. *Any spectator* (not *You*) *could tell by the way John caught the ball that his throw would be too late.*

your, you're   *Your* is a possessive pronoun; *you're* is a contraction of *you are. Is that your new motorcycle? You're on the list of finalists.*

W2

Wordy sentences

Long sentences are not necessarily wordy, nor are short sentences always concise. A sentence is wordy if its meaning can be conveyed in fewer words.

W2-a   Eliminate redundancies.

Redundancies such as *cooperate together, close proximity, basic essentials,* and *true fact* are a common source of wordiness. There is no need to say the same thing twice.

▶ Mr. Barker still hasn't paid last month's rent. ~~yet,~~
  _∧

▶ Black slaves were ~~called or~~ stereotyped as lazy even though they were the main labor force of the South.

Although modifiers ordinarily add meaning to the words they modify, occasionally they are redundant.

▶ Sylvia ~~very hurriedly~~ scribbled her name, address, and phone number on the back of a greasy napkin.

▶ Joel was determined ~~in his mind~~ to lose weight.

W2-b Avoid unnecessary repetition of words.

Although words may be repeated deliberately, for effect, repetitions will seem awkward if they are clearly unnecessary. When a more concise version is possible, choose it.

▶ Our fifth patient, in room six, is ~~a~~ mentally ill. ~~patient.~~
  _∧

▶ The best teachers help each student to ~~become a better student~~
  grow _∧
  both academically and emotionally.

W2-c Cut empty or inflated phrases.

An empty phrase can be cut with little or no loss of meaning. Common examples are introductory word groups that apologize or hedge: *in my opinion, I think that, it seems that, one must admit that,* and so on.

▶ ~~In my opinion, our~~ *Our* current policy in Central America is misguided
  _∧
  on several counts.

Inflated phrases can be reduced to a word or two without loss of meaning.

INFLATED	CONCISE
along the lines of	like
at this point in time	now
by means of	by
due to the fact that	because
for the purpose of	for
for the reason that	because
in order to	to
in spite of the fact that	although
in the event that	if
in the final analysis	finally
in the neighborhood of	about
until such time as	until

▶ We will file the appropriate papers ~~in the event that~~ *if* we are

unable to meet the deadline.

W2-d Simplify the structure.

If the structure of a sentence is needlessly indirect, try simplifying
it. Look for opportunities to strengthen the verb.

▶ The financial analyst claimed that because of volatile market

conditions she could not ~~make an~~ estimate ~~of~~ the company's future

profits.

The verb *estimate* is more vigorous and more concise than *make an
estimate of.*

The colorless verbs *is, are, was,* and *were* frequently generate
excess words.

▶ The administrative secretary ~~is responsible for monitoring and~~
monitors and balances

~~balancing~~ the budgets for travel, contract services, and personnel.

The constructions *there is* and *there are* (or *there was* and *there
were*) also generate excess words.

▶ ~~There is~~ *A*nother module ~~that~~ tells the story of Charles Darwin

and introduces the theory of evolution.

W2-e Reduce clauses to phrases, phrases to single words.

Word groups functioning as modifiers can often be made more compact. Look for any opportunities to reduce clauses to phrases or phrases to single words.

▶ Thermography, ~~which is~~ a new method of detecting breast cancer, records heat patterns on black-and-white or color-coded film.

▶ Susan's stylish jeans, ~~made of leather,~~ *leather* were too warm for our climate.

W3

Appropriate language

Language is appropriate when it suits your subject, conforms to the needs of your audience, and blends naturally with your own voice.

W3-a Stay away from jargon.

Jargon is specialized language used among members of a trade, profession, or group. Use jargon only when readers will be familiar with it; even then, use it only when plain English will not do as well.

JARGON   The indigenous body politic of South Africa has attempted to negotiate legal enfranchisement without result.

REVISED   The native population of South Africa has negotiated in vain for the right to vote.

Broadly defined, jargon includes puffed-up language designed more to impress readers than to inform them. Common examples in business, government, higher education, and the military are listed below, with plain English translations in parentheses.

ameliorate (improve)	indicator (sign)
commence (begin)	optimal (best, most favorable)
components (parts)	parameters (boundaries, limits)
endeavor (try)	peruse (read, look over)
exit (leave)	prior to (before)
facilitate (help)	utilize (use)
factor (consideration, cause)	viable (workable)
impact on (affect)	

Sentences filled with jargon are hard to read, and they are often wordy as well.

▶ All ~~employees functioning in the capacity of~~ work-study students *must prove that they are currently enrolled.* ~~are required to give evidence of current enrollment.~~

W3-b Avoid pretentious language and most euphemisms.

Hoping to sound profound or poetic, some writers embroider their thoughts with large words and flowery phrases, language that in fact sounds pretentious. Pretentious language is so ornate and often so wordy that it obscures the thought that lies beneath.

▶ When our *parents become old,* ~~progenitors reach their silver-haired and golden years,~~ we frequently *bury* ~~ensepulcher~~ them in *old-age* homes ~~for senescent beings~~ as if they were already among the *dead.* ~~deceased.~~

Euphemisms, nice-sounding words or phrases substituted for words thought to sound harsh or ugly, are sometimes appropriate. It is customary, for example, to say that a couple is "sleeping together" or that someone has "passed away." Most euphemisms, however, are needlessly evasive or even deceitful. Like pretentious language, they obscure the intended meaning.

EUPHEMISM	PLAIN ENGLISH
adult entertainment	pornography
preowned automobile	used car
economically deprived	poor
selected out	fired
negative savings	debts

EUPHEMISM	PLAIN ENGLISH
strategic withdrawal	retreat or defeat
revenue enhancers	taxes
chemical dependency	drug addiction

W3-c In most contexts, avoid slang and nonstandard English.

Slang is an informal and sometimes private vocabulary that expresses the solidarity of a group such as teenagers, rock musicians, or football fans; it is subject to more rapid change than standard English. For example, the slang teenagers use to express approval changes every few years; *cool, groovy, neat, wicked,* and *awesome* have replaced one another within the last three decades. Sometimes slang becomes so widespread that it is accepted as standard vocabulary. *Jazz,* for example, started as slang but is now generally accepted to describe a style of music.

Although slang has a certain vitality, it is a code that not everyone understands, and it is very informal. Therefore, it is inappropriate in most written work.

▶ If we don't begin studying for the final, a whole semester's work ~~is~~ *will be wasted.*
~~going down the tubes.~~

▶ The government's "filth" guidelines for food will ~~gross you out.~~ *disgust you.*

Standard English is the language used by educated people in all academic, business, and professional fields. Nonstandard English is spoken by people with a common regional or social heritage. Although nonstandard English may be appropriate when spoken within a close group, it is out of place in most formal and informal writing.

▶ The counselor ~~have~~ *has* so many problems in her own life that she
~~don't~~ *doesn't* know how to advise anyone else.

If you suspect that your writing has been influenced by nonstandard speech patterns, review Grammatical Sentences, especially G1 and G2, which describe the standard English forms of verbs. You might also scan the Glossary of Usage (W1), which contrasts many standard and nonstandard uses of language.

W3-d Choose an appropriate level of formality.

In deciding on a level of formality, consider both your subject and your audience. Does the subject demand a dignified treatment, or is a relaxed tone more suitable? Will the audience be put off if you assume too close a relationship with them, or might you alienate them by seeming too distant?

For most college and professional writing, some degree of formality is appropriate. In a letter applying for a job, for example, it is a mistake to sound too breezy and informal.

TOO INFORMAL	I'd like to get that receptionist's job you've got in the paper.
MORE FORMAL	I would like to apply for the receptionist's position listed in the *Peoria Journal Star*.

Informal writing is appropriate for private letters, business correspondence between close associates, articles in popular magazines, and personal narratives. In such writing, formal language can seem out of place.

▶ Once a pitcher for the Cincinnati Reds, Bob shared with me the secrets of his trade. His lesson ~~commenced~~ *began* with his famous curve ball, ~~implemented~~ *which he threw* by tucking the little finger behind the ball instead of holding it straight out. Next he ~~elucidated~~ *revealed* the mysteries of the sucker pitch, a slow ball coming behind a fast windup.

W3-e Avoid sexist language.

The pronouns *he, him,* and *his* were traditionally used to refer indefinitely to persons of either sex.

TRADITIONAL   A journalist is stimulated by *his* deadline.

Today, however, such usage is widely viewed as sexist because it excludes women and encourages sex-role stereotyping — the view that men are somehow more suited than women to be journalists, doctors, and so on.

One option, of course, is to substitute a pair of pronouns: *A journalist is stimulated by his or her deadline.* This strategy is fine in small doses, but it generates extra words that become awkward when repeated throughout an essay. A better strategy, many writers have discovered, is simply to write in the plural.

REVISED　　*Journalists* are stimulated by *their* deadlines.

Yet another strategy is to revise the sentence so that the problem does not arise.

REVISED　　A journalist is stimulated by *a* deadline.

Like the pronouns *he, him,* and *his,* the nouns *man* and *men* were once used indefinitely to refer to persons of either sex. Current usage demands gender-neutral terms instead.

INAPPROPRIATE	APPROPRIATE
chairman	chairperson, moderator, chair, head
clergyman	member of the clergy, minister, priest
congressman	member of Congress, representative, legislator
fireman	firefighter
foreman	supervisor
mailman	mail carrier, postal worker
mankind	people, humans
manpower	personnel
policeman	police officer
salesman	salesperson, sales associate
to man	to operate, to staff
weatherman	weather forecaster, meteorologist
workman	worker, laborer

W4

Exact language

Two reference works will help you find words to express your meaning exactly: a good dictionary (see W5) and a book of synonyms and antonyms such as *Roget's International Thesaurus.*

W4-a Select words with appropriate connotations.

In addition to their strict dictionary meanings (or *denotations*), words have *connotations,* emotional colorings that affect how readers respond to them. The word *steely* denotes "made of or resembling commercial iron that contains carbon," but it also calls up a cluster of images associated with steel, such as the sensation of touching it. These associations give the word its connotations — cold, smooth, unbending.

If the connotation of a word does not seem appropriate for your purpose, your audience, or your subject matter, the word should be changed. When a more appropriate word does not come quickly to mind, consult a dictionary or a thesaurus.

▶ The model was ~~skinny~~ *slender* and fashionable.

The connotation of the word *skinny* was too negative.

▶ As I covered the boats with marsh grass, the ~~perspiration~~ *sweat* I had worked up evaporated in the wind, making the cold morning air even colder.

The term *perspiration* was too dainty for the context, which suggested vigorous exercise.

W4-b Prefer specific, concrete nouns and active verbs.

Unlike general nouns, which refer to broad classes of things, specific nouns point to definite and particular items. *Film,* for example, names a general class, *horror film* names a narrower class, and *Carrie* is more specific still.

Unlike abstract nouns, which refer to qualities and ideas (*justice, beauty, realism, dignity*), concrete nouns point to immediate, often sensate experience and to physical objects (*steeple, asphalt, lilac, stone, garlic*).

Specific, concrete nouns express meaning more vividly than general or abstract ones. Although general and abstract language is sometimes necessary to convey your meaning, ordinarily prefer specific, concrete alternatives.

▶ The senator spoke about the challenges of the future: problems *of famine, pollution, dwindling resources, and arms control.* ~~concerning the environment and world peace.~~
∧

Nouns such as *thing, area, factor,* and *individual* are especially dull and imprecise.

rewards.

▶ A career in transportation management offers many ~~things.~~
∧

experienced technician.

▶ Try pairing a trainee with an ~~individual with technical experience.~~
∧

Like specific, concrete nouns, active verbs express meaning more vividly than their duller counterparts — forms of the verb *be* or verbs in the passive voice. Forms of the verb *be* (*be, am, is, are, was, were, being,* and *been*) lack color because they convey no action. Verbs in the passive voice lack vigor because their subjects receive the action instead of doing it. (See R2-b and G2-e.) Forms of *be* and passive verbs have legitimate uses, but if an active verb can convey your meaning, use it.

FORM OF BE | A surge of power *was* responsible for the destruction of the coolant pumps.

PASSIVE | The coolant pumps *were destroyed* by a surge of power.

REVISED ACTIVE | A surge of power *destroyed* the coolant pumps.

fluctuate without warning.

▶ The moods of a manic-depressive ~~are unpredictable.~~
∧

A bolt of lightning struck the transformer,

▶ ~~The transformer was struck by a bolt of lightning,~~ plunging us
∧
into darkness.

Even among active verbs, some are more active — and therefore more vigorous and colorful — than others. Carefully selected verbs can energize a piece of writing.

swept   *hooked*

▶ The goalie crouched low, ~~reached~~ out his stick, and ~~sent~~ the puck
∧   ∧
away from the mouth of the goal.

W4-c Do not misuse words.

If a word is not in your active vocabulary, you may find yourself misusing it, sometimes with embarrassing consequences. When in doubt, check the dictionary.

▶ The fans were ~~migrating~~ *climbing* up the bleachers in search of good seats.

▶ Mrs. Johnson tried to fight but to no ~~prevail~~ *avail.*

▶ Drugs have so ~~diffused~~ *permeated* our culture that they touch all segments of our society.

W4-d Use standard idioms.

Idioms are speech forms that follow no easily specified rules. The British say "Maria went *to hospital*," an idiom strange to American ears, which are accustomed to hearing *the* in front of *hospital*. Native speakers of a language seldom have problems with idioms, but prepositions sometimes cause trouble, especially when they follow certain verbs and adjectives. When in doubt, consult a good desk dictionary: Look up the word preceding the troublesome preposition.

UNIDIOMATIC	IDIOMATIC
abide with (a decision)	abide by (a decision)
according with	according to
agree to (an idea)	agree with (an idea)
angry at (a person)	angry with (a person)
capable to	capable of
comply to	comply with
desirous to	desirous of
different than	different from
intend on doing	intend to do
off of	off
plan on doing	plan to do
preferable than	preferable to
prior than	prior to
superior than	superior to
sure and	sure to
try and	try to
type of a	type of

W4-e Avoid clichés.

The pioneer who first announced that he had "slept like a log" no doubt amused his companions with a fresh and unlikely comparison. Today, however, that comparison is a cliché, a saying that has lost its dazzle from overuse. No longer can it surprise.

To see just how predictable clichés are, put your hand over the right-hand column below and then finish the phrases on the left.

cool as a	cucumber
beat around	the bush
blind as a	bat
busy as a	bee
crystal	clear
dead as a	doornail
from the frying pan	into the fire
light as a	feather
like a bull	in a china shop
playing with	fire
nutty as a	fruitcake
selling like	hotcakes
starting out at the bottom	of the ladder
water over the	dam
white as a	sheet, ghost
avoid clichés like the	plague

The cure for clichés is frequently simple: Just delete them. When this won't work, try adding some element of surprise. One woman, for example, who had written that she had butterflies in her stomach, revised her cliché like this:

> If all of the action in my stomach is caused by butterflies, there must be a horde of them, with horseshoes on.

The image of butterflies wearing horseshoes is fresh and unlikely, not dully predictable like the original cliché.

W4-f Use figures of speech with care.

A figure of speech is an expression that uses words imaginatively (rather than literally) to make abstract ideas concrete. Most often, figures of speech compare two seemingly unlike things to reveal surprising similarities.

In a *simile,* the writer makes the comparison explicitly, usually by introducing it with *like* or *as:* "By the time cotton had to be picked, grandfather's neck was as red as the clay he plowed." In a *metaphor,* the *like* or *as* is omitted, and the comparison is implied. For example, in the Old Testament Song of Solomon, a young woman compares the man she loves to a fruit tree: "With great delight I sat in his shadow, and his fruit was sweet to my taste."

Writers sometimes use figures of speech without thinking carefully about the images they evoke. This can result in a *mixed metaphor,* the combination of two or more images that don't make sense together.

▶ Crossing Utah's salt flats in his new Corvette, my father flew *at jet speed.* ~~under a full head of steam.~~
     ∧

▶ Our office had decided to put all controversial issues on a back

  burner. ~~in a holding pattern.~~
     ∧

W5

The dictionary

A good desk dictionary — such as *The American Heritage Dictionary of the English Language, The Random House College Dictionary,* or *Webster's New Collegiate* or *New World Dictionary of the American Language* — is an indispensable writer's aid.

A sample dictionary entry, taken from *The American Heritage Dictionary,* appears on page 109. Labels show where various kinds of information about a word can be found in that dictionary.

Spelling, word division, pronunciation

The main entry (*pre·vent* in the sample entry) shows the correct spelling of the word. When there are two correct spellings of a word (*preventable, preventible*), both are given, with the preferred spelling appearing first.

The main entry also shows how the word is divided into syllables. The dot between *pre* and *vent* separates the word's two syllables. When a word is compound, the main entry shows how to

Pronunciation — Grammatical label

Word division — Word endings — Meanings

Spelling ——— **pre·vent** (pri-věnt′) *v.* **-vented, -venting, -vents.** —*tr.* **1.** To keep from happening, as by some prior action; avert; thwart. **2.** To keep (someone) from doing something; hinder; impede. Often used with *from.* **3.** *Obsolete.* To anticipate or counter in advance: *"Your goodness still prevents my wishes."* (Dryden).
Usage — **4.** *Obsolete.* To come before; precede. —*intr.* To present an label obstacle: *There will be a picnic, if nothing prevents.* [Middle English *preventen,* to anticipate, from Latin *praevenire,* to come before, anticipate : *prae-,* before + *venire,* to come (see **gwā-** in Appendix*).] —**pre·vent′a·bil′i·ty, pre·vent′i·bil′i·ty** *n.* —**pre·vent′a·ble, pre·vent′i·ble** *adj.* —**pre·vent′er** *n.*

Synonyms — **Synonyms:** *prevent, preclude, obviate, forestall.* These verbs refer to stopping or hindering an action or eliminating a situation or condition that could produce an action. *Prevent* strongly implies decisive counteraction to stop something from happening. *Preclude* makes an event or action impossible or largely ineffectual by removing the conditions for it, while *obviate* makes an event or action unnecessary in the same way. *Forestall* less forcefully implies anticipatory action to prevent or hinder an imminent happening, but not by eliminating the conditions for it.

Usage — **Usage:** *Prevent* is often followed by a gerund. A noun or pronoun preceding the gerund is in the possessive case: *We tried to prevent Jim's leaving* (not *Jim leaving*). Such examples can also be expressed: *We tried to prevent Jim from leaving. She prevented them from moving.*

Word origin (etymology)

write the word: as one word (*crossroad*), as a hyphenated word (*cross-stitch*), or as two words (*cross section*).

The word's pronunciation is given just after the main entry. The accents indicate which syllables are stressed; the other marks are explained in the dictionary's pronunciation key. In most dictionaries this key appears at the bottom of every page or every other page.

Word endings and grammatical labels

When a word takes endings to indicate grammatical functions (called *inflections*), the endings are listed in boldface, as with *-vented, -venting,* and *-vents* in the sample entry.

Labels for the parts of speech and for other grammatical terms are abbreviated. The most commonly used abbreviations are these:

n.	noun	adj.	adjective
pl.	plural	adv.	adverb
sing.	singular	pron.	pronoun
v.	verb	prep.	preposition
tr.	transitive verb	conj.	conjunction
intr.	intransitive verb	interj.	interjection

Meanings, word origin, synonyms, and antonyms

Each meaning for the word is given a number. Occasionally a word's use is illustrated in a quoted sentence, as with the sentence by Dryden in the sample entry.

The origin of the word, called its *etymology,* appears in brackets after the list of meanings (in some dictionaries it appears before the meanings).

Synonyms, words similar in meaning to the main entry, are frequently listed. In the sample entry, the dictionary draws distinctions in meaning among the various synonyms. Antonyms, which do not appear in the sample entry, are words having a meaning opposite from that of the main entry.

Usage

Usage labels indicate when, where, or under what conditions a particular meaning for a word is appropriately used. Common labels are *informal* (or *colloquial*), *slang, nonstandard, dialect, obsolete, archaic, poetic,* and *British*. In the sample entry, two meanings of *prevent* are labeled as *obsolete* because they are no longer in use.

Dictionaries sometimes include usage notes as well. In the sample entry, the dictionary offers advice on a grammatical problem that sometimes arises following the verb *prevent*. Such advice is based on the opinions of many experts and on actual usage in current magazines, newspapers, and books.

Punctuation

P

Punctuation

P1

The comma

The comma was invented to help readers. Without it, sentence parts can collide into one another unexpectedly, causing misreadings.

> CONFUSING   If you cook Elmer will do the dishes.
>
> CONFUSING   While we were eating a rattlesnake approached our campsite.

Add commas in the logical places (after *cook* and *eating*), and suddenly all is clear. No longer is Elmer being cooked, the rattlesnake being eaten.

Various rules have evolved to prevent such misreadings and to speed readers along through complex grammatical structures. Those rules are detailed in this section.

P1-a Use a comma before a coordinating conjunction joining independent clauses.

When a coordinating conjunction connects two or more independent clauses — word groups that could stand alone as separate sentences — a comma must precede it. There are seven coordinating conjunctions in English: *and, but, or, nor, for, so,* and *yet.*

A comma tells readers that one independent clause has come to a close and that another is about to begin.

▶ Nearly everyone has heard of love at first sight ‸, but I fell in love

at first dance.

EXCEPTION: If the two independent clauses are short and there is no danger of misreading, the comma may be omitted.

> The plane took off and we were on our way.

CAUTION: Do *not* use a comma to separate compound elements that are not independent clauses. See P2-a.

▶ A good money manager controls expenses,/ and invests surplus

dollars to meet future needs.

The word group following *and* is not an independent clause but is the second half of a compound predicate.

P1-b Use a comma after an introductory word group.

The most common introductory word groups are clauses and phrases functioning as adverbs. Such word groups usually tell when, where, how, why, or under what conditions the main action of the sentence occurred. (See R3-a, R3-b, and R3-e.)

A comma tells readers that the introductory clause or phrase has come to a close and that the main part of the sentence is about to begin.

▶ When Irwin was ready to eat, his cat jumped onto the table.

▶ Near a small stream at the bottom of the canyon, we discovered

an abandoned shelter.

EXCEPTION: The comma may be omitted after a short adverb clause or phrase if there is no danger of misreading.

In no time we were at 2,800 feet.

Sentences also frequently begin with participial phrases describing the noun or pronoun immediately following them. The comma tells readers that they are about to learn the identity of the person or thing described; therefore, the comma is usually required even when the phrase is short. (See R3-b.)

▶ Knowing that he couldn't outrun a car, Kevin took to the fields.

▶ Excited about the move, Alice and Don began packing their books.

NOTE: Other introductory word groups include conjunctive adverbs, transitional expressions, and absolute phrases. (See P1-f.)

P1-c Use a comma between all items in a series.

When three or more items are presented in a series, those items should be separated from one another with commas. Items in a series may be single words, phrases, or clauses.

At Dominique's one can order fillet of rattlesnake, bison burgers, or pickled eel.

Although some writers view the comma between the last two items as optional, most experts advise using it because its omission can result in ambiguity or misreading.

▶ My uncle willed me all of his property, houses‚ and warehouses.
                                                    ∧

Did the uncle will his property *and* houses *and* warehouses—or simply his property, consisting of houses and warehouses? If the first meaning is intended, a comma is necessary to prevent ambiguity.

▶ The activities include a search for lost treasure, dubious financial

dealings, much discussion of ancient heresies‚ and midnight
                                                ∧

orgies.

Without the comma this sentence is easily misread. The activities seem to include discussion of orgies, not participation in them. The comma makes it clear that *midnight orgies* is a separate item in the series.

P1-d Use a comma between coordinate adjectives not joined by a coordinating conjunction. Do not use a comma between cumulative adjectives.

When two or more adjectives each modify a noun separately, they are *coordinate*.

Mother has become a *strong, confident, independent* woman.

Adjectives are coordinate if they can be joined with *and* (strong *and* confident *and* independent) or if they can be scrambled (an independent, strong, confident woman).

Adjectives that do not modify the noun separately are cumulative.

Three large gray shapes moved slowly toward us.

Beginning with the adjective closest to the noun *shapes,* these modifiers lean on one another, piggyback style, with each modifying a larger word group. *Gray* modifies *shapes, large* modifies *gray shapes,* and *three* modifies *large gray shapes*. We cannot insert the word *and* between cumulative adjectives (three *and* large *and* gray shapes). Nor can we scramble them (gray three large shapes).

COORDINATE ADJECTIVES

▶ Robert is a warm, gentle, affectionate father.

CUMULATIVE ADJECTIVES

▶ Ira ordered a rich/ chocolate/ layer cake.

P1-e Use commas to set off nonrestrictive word groups. Do not use commas to set off restrictive word groups.

Word groups describing nouns or pronouns (adjective clauses, adjective phrases, and appositives) are restrictive or nonrestrictive. A *restrictive* element defines or limits the meaning of the word it modifies and is therefore essential to the meaning of the sentence. Because it contains essential information, a restrictive element is not set off with commas.

RESTRICTIVE
For camp the children needed clothes *that were washable*.

If you remove a restrictive element from a sentence, the meaning changes significantly, becoming more general than you intended. The writer of the example sentence does not mean that the children needed clothes in general. The intended meaning is more limited: The children needed *washable* clothes.

A *nonrestrictive* element describes a noun or pronoun whose meaning has already been clearly defined or limited. Because it contains nonessential or parenthetical information, a nonrestrictive element is set off with commas.

NONRESTRICTIVE
For camp the children needed sturdy shoes, *which were expensive*.

If you remove a nonrestrictive element from a sentence, the meaning does not change dramatically. Some meaning is lost, to be sure, but the defining characteristics of the person or thing described remain the same as before. The children needed *sturdy shoes,* and these happened to be expensive.

Often it is difficult to tell whether a word group is restrictive or nonrestrictive without seeing it in context and considering your meaning. Should you write "The dessert made with fresh raspberries was delicious" or "The dessert, made with fresh raspberries, was delicious"? That depends. If the phrase *made with fresh raspberries* tells readers which of several desserts you're referring to, you would omit the commas. If the phrase merely adds information about the one dessert served with the meal, you would use the commas.

Adjective clauses

Adjective clauses are patterned like sentences, containing subjects and verbs, but they function within sentences as modifiers of nouns or pronouns. Adjective clauses begin with a relative pronoun (*who, whom, whose, which, that*) or with a relative adverb (*where, when*).

NONRESTRICTIVE CLAUSE

▶ Ed's country house, which is located on thirteen acres, was completely furnished with bats in the rafters and mice in the kitchen.

The clause *which is located on thirteen acres* does not restrict the meaning of *Ed's country house,* so the information is nonessential and is set off with commas.

RESTRICTIVE CLAUSE

▶ An office manager for a corporation that had government contracts asked her supervisor whether she could reprimand her co-workers for smoking.

Because the adjective clause *that had government contracts* identifies the corporation, the information is essential.

NOTE: Many writers reserve *which* for nonrestrictive clauses and *that* for restrictive clauses.

Phrases functioning as adjectives

Prepositional or verbal phrases functioning as adjectives may be restrictive or nonrestrictive and are punctuated according to the rules used for adjective clauses.

NONRESTRICTIVE PHRASE

▶ The helicopter, with its 100,000-candlepower spotlight

illuminating the area, circled above.

The *with* phrase is nonessential because its purpose is not to specify which of two or more helicopters is being discussed.

RESTRICTIVE PHRASE

▶ One corner of the attic was filled with newspapers / dating from

the turn of the century.

Dating from the turn of the century restricts the meaning of *newspapers,* so the comma should be omitted.

Appositives

An appositive is a noun phrase that renames a nearby noun. Most appositives are nonrestrictive and should be set off with commas; the few that are restrictive require no commas.

NONRESTRICTIVE APPOSITIVE

▶ Norman Mailer's first novel, *The Naked and the Dead,* was a best-

seller.

The term *first* restricts the meaning to one novel, so the appositive *The Naked and the Dead* is nonrestrictive.

RESTRICTIVE APPOSITIVE

▶ The song / "Fire It Up / " was blasted out of amplifiers ten feet tall.

Once they've read *song,* readers still don't know precisely which song the writer means. The appositive following *song* restricts its meaning.

P1-f Use commas to set off conjunctive adverbs, transitional expressions, parenthetical expressions, absolute phrases, and contrasted elements.

Conjunctive adverbs and transitional expressions

Conjunctive adverbs such as *however, therefore, moreover,* and *nevertheless* and transitional expressions such as *for example, as a matter of fact,* and *in other words* serve as bridges between sentences or between the independent clauses of a compound sentence.

When a conjunctive adverb or transitional expression appears between independent clauses in a compound sentence, it is preceded by a semicolon and is usually followed by a comma. (See P3-a.)

▶ Minh did not understand our language; moreover, he was

unfamiliar with our customs.

▶ Natural foods are not always salt free; for example, celery

contains more sodium than most people would imagine.

When a conjunctive adverb or transitional expression appears at the beginning of a sentence or in the middle of an independent clause, it is usually set off with commas.

▶ As a matter of fact, American football was established by fans who

wanted to play a more organized game of football.

▶ The prospective babysitter looked very promising; she was busy,

however, throughout the month of January.

EXCEPTION: If a conjunctive adverb or transitional expression blends smoothly with the rest of the sentence, calling for little or no pause in reading, it does not need to be set off with a comma.

Bill's typewriter is broken; *therefore* you will need to borrow Sue's.

Parenthetical expressions

Expressions that are distinctly parenthetical should be set off with commas. Providing supplemental comments or information, they interrupt the flow of a sentence or appear as afterthoughts.

▶ Evolution, so far as we know, doesn't work this way.

▶ The striped bass weighed about twelve pounds, give or take a few ounces.

Absolute phrases

Absolute phrases should be set off with commas. An absolute phrase, which modifies the whole sentence, usually consists of a noun followed by a participle or participial phrase. (See R3-d.)

▶ His tennis game at last perfected, Chris won the cup.

▶ Brenda was forced to rely on public transportation, her car having been wrecked the week before.

Contrasted elements

Sharp contrasts beginning with words such as *not* and *unlike* are set off with commas.

▶ Now that I am married Jane talks to me as an adult, not as her little sister.

▶ Celia, unlike Robert, had no loathing for dance contests.

P1-g Use commas to set off nouns of direct address, the words *yes* and *no*, interrogative tags, and mild interjections.

▶ Forgive us, Dr. Spock, for spanking Brian.

▶ Yes, the loan will probably be approved.

▶ The film was faithful to the book, wasn't it?

▶ Well, cases like these are difficult to decide.

P1-h Use commas with expressions such as *he said* to set off direct quotations. (See also P6-e.)

▶ Naturalist Arthur Cleveland Bent remarked, "In part the peregrine declined unnoticed because it is not adorable."

▶ "Convictions are more dangerous foes of truth than lies, " wrote philosopher Friedrich Nietzsche.

P1-i Use commas with dates, addresses, and titles.

In dates, the year is set off from the rest of the sentence with a pair of commas.

▶ On December 12, 1890, orders were sent out for the arrest of Sitting Bull.

EXCEPTIONS: Commas are not needed if the date is inverted or if only the month and year are given.

On 15 April 1988 both houses of Congress voted on important legislation.

January 1987 was an extremely cold month.

The elements of an address or place name are followed by commas. A zip code, however, is not preceded by a comma.

▶ John Lennon was born in Liverpool, England, in 1940.

▶ Please send the package to Greg Tarvin at 708 Spring Street, Washington, Illinois 61571.

If a title follows a name, separate it from the rest of the sentence with a pair of commas.

▶ Sandra Barnes, M.D., performed the surgery.

P2

Unnecessary commas

P2-a Do not use a comma between compound elements that are not independent clauses.

Although a comma should be used before a coordinating conjunction joining independent clauses (see P1-a), this rule should not be extended to other compound word groups.

▶ The director led the cast members to their positions⁄ and gave an

inspiring last-minute pep talk.

The word group following *and* is not an independent clause; *and* connects the verbs *led* and *gave*.

▶ Jake still does not realize that his illness is serious⁄ and that he

will have to alter his diet to improve.

The word group following *and* is not an independent clause. *And* connects two subordinate clauses, each beginning with *that*.

P2-b Do not use a comma to separate a verb from its subject or object.

A sentence should flow from subject to verb to object without unnecessary pauses. Commas may appear between these major sentence elements only when a specific rule calls for them.

▶ Abiding by the 55-mile-per-hour speed limit⁄ can save gasoline.

▶ Fran explained to him⁄ that she was busy and would see him later.

P2-c Do not use a comma before the first or after the last item in a series.

Though commas are required between items in a series (see P1-c), do not place them either before or after the series.

▶ Other causes of asthmatic attacks are/ stress, change in

temperature, humidity, and cold air.

▶ Ironically, this job that appears so glamorous, carefree, and easy/

carries a high degree of responsibility.

P2-d Do not use a comma between cumulative adjectives or between an adjective and the noun that follows it.

Though commas are required between coordinate adjectives (those that can be separated with *and*), they do not belong between cumulative adjectives (those that cannot be separated with *and*). For a full discussion, see P1-d.

▶ In the corner of the closet we found an old/ maroon hatbox from

Sears.

A comma should never be used to separate an adjective from the noun that follows it.

▶ It was a senseless, dangerous/ mission.

P2-e Do not use commas to set off restrictive or mildly parenthetical elements.

Restrictive elements are modifiers or appositives necessary for identifying the nouns they follow; therefore, they are essential to the meaning of the sentence and should not be set off with commas. For a full discussion, see P1-e.

▶ Drivers/ who think they own the road/ make cycling a dangerous

sport.

The *who* clause restricts the meaning of *Drivers* and is therefore essential to the meaning of the sentence. The writer who puts commas around the *who* clause falsely suggests that all drivers think they own the road and that all drivers make cycling a dangerous sport.

▶ Margaret Mead's book ╱ *Coming of Age in Samoa* ╱ stirred up

considerable controversy when it was published.

Since Margaret Mead wrote more than one book, the appositive contains information essential to the meaning of the sentence.

Although commas should be used with distinctly parenthetical expressions (see P1-f), do not use them to set off elements that are only mildly parenthetical.

▶ As long as patients are treated in a professional yet compassionate

manner, most ╱ eventually ╱ learn to deal with their illness.

P2-f Do not use a comma before a parenthesis.

▶ At MCI Sylvia began at the bottom ╱ (with only three and a half

walls and a swivel chair), but now she is a supervisor.

P3

The semicolon

The semicolon is used to separate major sentence elements of equal grammatical rank.

P3-a Use a semicolon between closely related independent clauses not joined by a coordinating conjunction.

When related independent clauses appear in one sentence, they are ordinarily connected with a comma and a coordinating conjunction (*and, but, or, nor, for, so, yet*). The coordinating conjunction expresses the relation between the clauses. If the relation is clear without the conjunction, a writer may choose to connect the clauses with a semicolon instead.

> Injustice is relatively easy to bear; what stings is justice.
> —H. L. Mencken

The semicolon must be used whenever the coordinating conjunction has been omitted between independent clauses. This rule applies even when the independent clauses have been joined with a conjunctive adverb such as *however, nevertheless, moreover,* or *therefore* or a transitional expression such as *in fact* or *for example.* To use merely a comma creates an error known as a comma splice. (See G6.)

▶ Evita didn't rise through hard work and dedication/; she found other means.

▶ I learned all the rules and regulations/; however, I never really learned to control the ball.

P3-b Use a semicolon between items in a series containing internal punctuation.

▶ Classic science fiction sagas are *Star Trek,* with Mr. Spock and his large pointed ears/; *Battlestar Galactica,* with its Cylon Raiders/; and *Star Wars,* with Han Solo, Luke Skywalker, and Darth Vader.

Without the semicolons the reader must sort out the major groupings, distinguishing between important and less important pauses according to the logic of the sentence. By inserting semicolons at the major breaks, the writer does this work for the reader.

P3-c Avoid common misuses of the semicolon.

Do not use a semicolon to separate a subordinate clause from the rest of the sentence. The semicolon should be used only between items of equal rank.

▶ Unless you brush your teeth within ten or fifteen minutes after

eating, brushing does almost no good.

As a rule, do not use a semicolon between independent clauses when those clauses have been joined with a coordinating conjunction (*and, but, or, nor, for, so, yet*).

▶ Twenty-eight of the applicants had college degrees, but most of

them were clearly unqualified for the position.

EXCEPTION: If at least one of the independent clauses contains internal punctuation, a writer may choose to use a semicolon even though the clauses are joined with a coordinating conjunction.

> As a vehicle [the model T] was hard-working, commonplace, and heroic; and it often seemed to transmit those qualities to the persons who rode in it.   —E. B. White

Although a comma would also be correct in this sentence, the semicolon is more effective, for it indicates the relative weights of the pauses.

P4

The colon

The colon is used primarily to call attention to the words that follow it.

P4-a Use a colon after an independent clause to direct attention to a list, an appositive, or a quotation.

A LIST
The daily routine should include at least the following: twenty knee bends, fifty sit-ups, fifteen leg lifts, and five minutes of running in place.

AN APPOSITIVE
My roommate is guilty of two of the seven deadly sins: gluttony and sloth.

A QUOTATION
Consider the words of John F. Kennedy: "Ask not what your country can do for you; ask what you can do for your country."

For other ways of introducing quotations, see P6-e.

P4-b Use a colon between independent clauses if the second summarizes or explains the first.

Faith is like love: It cannot be forced.

NOTE: When an independent clause follows a colon, it may begin with a lowercase or a capital letter.

P4-c Use a colon after the salutation in a formal letter, to indicate hours and minutes, to show proportions, and to separate city and date in bibliographic entries.

Dear Sir or Madam:

5:30 P.M. (or p.m.)

Martinis should be mixed about 5:1.

New York: St. Martin's, 1989

P4-d Avoid common misuses of the colon.

Do not insert a colon between a verb and its object or complement or between a preposition and its object. A colon must be preceded by a full independent clause.

▶ Some important vitamins found in vegetables are꞉/ vitamin A, thiamine, niacin, and vitamin C.

▶ The area to be painted consisted of꞉/ three gable ends, trim work, sixteen windows, and a front and back porch.

P5

The apostrophe

P5-a Use an apostrophe to indicate that a noun is possessive.

Possessive nouns usually indicate ownership, as in *Tim's hat* or *the lawyer's desk*. Frequently, however, ownership is only loosely implied: *the tree's roots, a day's work*. If you are not sure whether a noun is possessive, try turning it into an *of* phrase: *the roots of the tree, the work of a day*.

When to add -'s

1. If the noun does not end in *-s,* add *-'s.*

Roy managed to climb out on the driver's side.

Thank you for refunding the children's money.

2. If the noun is singular and ends in *-s,* add *-'s.*

Lois's sister spent last year in India.

EXCEPTION: If pronunciation would be awkward with the added *-'s,* some writers use only the apostrophe. Either use is acceptable.

Euripides' plays are among my favorites.

When to add only an apostrophe

If the noun is plural and ends in *-s,* add only an apostrophe.

Both actresses' jewels were stolen.

Joint possession

To show joint possession, use *-'s* (or *-s'*) with the last noun only; to show individual possession, make all nouns possessive.

Have you seen Joyce and Greg's new camper?

John's and Marie's expectations of marriage couldn't have been more different.

In the first sentence, Joyce and Greg jointly own one camper. In the second sentence, John and Marie individually have different expectations.

Compound nouns

If a noun is compound, use *-'s* (or *-s'*) with the last element.

Her father-in-law's sculpture won first place.

P5-b Use an apostrophe and *-s* to indicate that an indefinite pronoun is possessive.

Indefinite pronouns are pronouns that refer to no specific person or thing: *everyone, someone, no one, something.* (See R1-b.)

Someone's raincoat has been left behind.

This diet will improve almost anyone's health.

P5-c Use an apostrophe to mark contractions.

In contractions the apostrophe takes the place of missing letters.

If that's not love, what would you call it?

Doesn't Frank plan to go on the tour?

That's stands for *that is, doesn't* for *does not.*

P5-d Use an apostrophe and *-s* to pluralize numbers mentioned as numbers, letters mentioned as letters, words mentioned as words, and abbreviations.

Peggy skated nearly perfect figure 8's.

The bleachers in our section were marked with large red *J*'s.

We've heard enough *maybe*'s.

You must ask to see their I.D.'s.

EXCEPTION: An *-s* alone is often added to the years in a decade: the *1980s.*

P5-e Avoid common misuses of the apostrophe.

1. Do not use an apostrophe with nouns that are not possessive.

▶ Some *outpatients*
outpatient's are given special parking permits.

2. Do not use an apostrophe in the possessive pronouns *its, whose, his, hers, ours, yours,* and *theirs.*

▶ Each area has *its*
it's own conference room.

It's means *it is.* The possessive pronoun *its* contains no apostrophe, despite the fact that it is possessive.

▶ This course was taught by a professional florist *whose*
who's technique was oriental.

Who's means *who is.* The possessive pronoun is *whose.*

P6

Quotation marks

P6-a Use quotation marks to enclose direct quotations.

Direct quotations of a person's words, whether spoken or written, must be in quotation marks.

> In a husky voice, Muhammad Ali bragged, "My opponent will be on the floor in round four. He'll take a dive in round five. In round nine he'll be all mine."

> "A foolish consistency is the hobgoblin of little minds," wrote Ralph Waldo Emerson.

CAUTION: Do not use quotation marks around indirect quotations. An indirect quotation reports someone's ideas without using that person's exact words.

> Ralph Waldo Emerson believed that consistency is the mark of a small mind.

EXCEPTION: Quotation marks are not used around long quotations that have been set off from the rest of the text. (See page 174.)

NOTE: In dialogue, begin a new paragraph to mark a change in speaker.

> "Mom, his name is Willie, not William. A thousand times I've told you, it's *Willie*."
> "Willie is a derivative of William, Lester. Surely his birth certificate doesn't have Willie on it, and I like calling people by their proper names."
> "Yes, it does, ma'am. My mother named me Willie K. Mason."
> —Gloria Naylor

If a single speaker utters more than one paragraph, introduce each paragraph with quotation marks, but do not use closing quotation marks until the end of the speech.

P6-b Use single quotation marks to enclose a quotation within a quotation.

> According to Paul Eliott, Eskimo hunters "chant an ancient magic song to the seal they are after: 'Beast of the sea! Come and place yourself before me in the early morning!' "

P6-c Use quotation marks around the titles of newspaper and magazine articles, poems, short stories, songs, television and radio programs, and chapters or subdivisions of books.

> Katherine Mansfield's "The Garden Party" provoked a lively discussion in our short-story class last night.

NOTE: Titles of books, plays, and films and names of magazines and newspapers are put in italics or underlined. (See M4-a.)

P6-d Quotation marks may be used to set off words used as words.

Although words used as words are ordinarily underlined to indicate italics (see M4-d), quotation marks are also acceptable.

> The words "flaunt" and "flout" are frequently confused.

> The words *flaunt* and *flout* are frequently confused.

P6-e Use punctuation with quotation marks according to convention.

This section describes the conventions used by American publishers in placing various marks of punctuation inside or outside quotation marks. It also explains how to punctuate when introducing quoted material.

Periods and commas

Always place periods and commas inside quotation marks.

> "This is a stick-up," said the well-dressed young couple. "We want all your money."

This rule applies to single quotation marks as well as double quotation marks. (See P6-b.) It also applies to all uses of quotation marks: for quoted material, for titles of works, and for words used as words.

Colons and semicolons

Put colons and semicolons outside quotation marks.

> Harold wrote, "I regret that I am unable to attend the fundraiser for AIDS research"; his letter, however, contained a substantial contribution.

Question marks and exclamation points

Put question marks and exclamation points inside quotation marks unless they apply to the sentence as a whole.

Contrary to tradition, bedtime at my house is marked by "Mommy, can I tell you a story now?"

Have you heard the old proverb "Do not climb the hill until you reach it"?

In the first sentence, the question mark applies only to the quoted question. In the second sentence, the question mark applies to the whole sentence.

Introducing quoted material

After a word group introducing a quotation, choose a colon, a comma, or no punctuation at all, whichever is appropriate in context.

If a quotation has been formally introduced, a colon is appropriate. A formal introduction is a full independent clause, not just an expression such as *he said* or *she remarked*.

Freuchen points out that the diet is not as monotonous as it may seem: "When you have meat and meat, and meat again, you learn to distinguish between the different parts of an animal."

If a quotation is introduced with an expression such as *he said* or *she remarked* — or if it is followed by such an expression — a comma is needed.

Robert Frost said, "You can be a little ungrammatical if you come from the right part of the country."

"You can be a little ungrammatical if you come from the right part of the country," Robert Frost said.

When a quotation is blended into the writer's own sentence, either a comma or no punctuation is appropriate, depending on the way in which the quotation fits into the sentence structure.

The future champion could, as he put it, "float like a butterfly and sting like a bee."

Charles Hudson noted that the prisoners escaped "by squeezing through a tiny window eighteen feet above the floor of their cell."

If a quotation appears at the beginning of a sentence, set it off with a comma unless the quotation ends with a question mark or an exclamation point.

"We shot them like dogs," boasted Davy Crockett, who was among Jackson's troops.

"What is it?" I asked, bracing myself.

If a quoted sentence is interrupted by explanatory words, use commas to set off the explanatory words.

"A great many people think they are thinking," wrote William James, "when they are merely rearranging their prejudices."

If two successive quoted sentences from the same source are interrupted by explanatory words, use a comma before the explanatory words and a period after them.

"I was a flop as a daily reporter," admitted E. B. White. "Every piece had to be a masterpiece—and before you knew it, Tuesday was Wednesday."

P6-f Avoid common misuses of quotation marks.

Do not use quotation marks to draw attention to familiar slang or to justify an attempt at humor.

▶ Greasers shout at their mothers, cruise the streets at night, and punch each other out /"just for fun."

Do not use quotation marks around indirect quotations. (See P6-a.)

P7

End punctuation

P7-a The period

1. Use a period to end all sentences except direct questions or genuine exclamations.

Everyone knows that a period should be used to end most sentences. The only problems that arise concern the choice between a period and a question mark or between a period and an exclamation point.

If a sentence reports a question instead of asking it directly, it should end with a period, not a question mark.

Celia asked whether the picnic would be canceled.

If a declarative or an imperative sentence is not a genuine exclamation, it should end with a period, not an exclamation point.

After years of working her way through school, Pat finally graduated with high honors.

Fill out the travel form in triplicate and then send it to the main office.

2. Use periods in abbreviations according to convention. A period is conventionally used in abbreviations such as the following:

Dr.	M.A.	A.M. (or a.m.)	i.e.
Mr.	Ph.D.	B.C. (or BC)	e.g.
Ms.	R.N.	A.D. (or AD)	etc.

A period is not used with U.S. Postal Service abbreviations for states: MD, TX, CA.

Ordinarily a period is not used in abbreviations of organization names:

NATO	UNESCO	AFL-CIO	FCC
TVA	IRS	SEC	IBM
USA	NAACP	PUSH	FTC
(or U.S.A.)	UCLA	NBA	NIH

Usage varies, however. When in doubt, consult a dictionary, a style manual, or a publication by the agency in question. Even the yellow pages can help.

P7-b The question mark

1. Use a question mark after a direct question.

Obviously a direct question should be followed by a question mark.

What is the horsepower of a 747 engine?

If a polite request is written in the form of a question, it too is usually followed by a question mark.

Would you please send me your catalog of lilies?

CAUTION: Do not use a question mark after an indirect question (one that is reported rather than asked directly). Use a period instead.

He asked me who was teaching the mythology course.

2. Questions in a series may be followed by question marks even when they are not complete sentences.

We wondered where Calamity had hidden this time. Under the sink? Behind the furnace? On top of the bookcase?

P7-c The exclamation point

1. Use an exclamation point after a word group or sentence that expresses exceptional feeling or deserves special emphasis.

The medic shook me and kept yelling, "He's dead! He's dead! Can't you see that?"

2. Do not overuse the exclamation point.

▶ In the fisherman's memory the fish lives on, increasing in length

and weight with each passing year, until at last it is big enough to

shade a fishing boat!̷.

This sentence doesn't need to be pumped up with an exclamation point. It is emphatic enough without it.

▶ Whenever I see Martina lunging forward to put away an overhead

smash, it might as well be me!̷.She does it just the way that I

would!

The first exclamation point should be deleted so that the second one will have more force.

P8

Other punctuation marks: the dash, parentheses, brackets, the ellipsis mark, the slash

P8-a The dash

When typing, use two hyphens to form a dash (--). Do not put spaces before or after the dash.

1. Use dashes to set off parenthetical material that deserves emphasis.

> Everything that went wrong—from the peeping Tom at her window to my head-on collision—was blamed on our move.

2. Use dashes to set off appositives that contain commas.

An appositive is a noun or noun phrase that renames a nearby noun. Ordinarily most appositives are set off with commas (see P1-e), but when the appositive contains commas, a pair of dashes helps readers see the relative importance of all the pauses.

> In my hometown the basic needs of people—food, clothing, and shelter—are less costly than in Los Angeles.

3. Use a dash to prepare for a list, a restatement, an amplification, or a dramatic shift in tone or thought.

> Along the wall are the bulk liquids—sesame seed oil, honey, safflower oil, and that half-liquid "peanuts only" peanut butter.

> Consider the amount of sugar in the average person's diet—104 pounds per year, 90 percent more than that consumed by our ancestors.

> Everywhere we looked there were little kids—a box of Cracker Jacks in one hand and mommy's or daddy's sleeve in the other.

> Kiere took a few steps back, came running full speed, kicked a mighty kick—and missed the ball.

4. Do not overuse the dash.

Unless there is a specific reason for using the dash, avoid it. Unnecessary dashes create a choppy effect.

▶ Seeing that our young people learn to use computers as

instructional tools∕for information retrieval∕makes good sense.

Herding them∕sheeplike∕into computer technology does not.

P8-b Parentheses

1. Use parentheses to enclose supplemental material, minor digressions, and afterthoughts.

> After taking her temperature, pulse, and blood pressure (routine vital signs), the nurse made Becky as comfortable as possible.

> The weights James was first able to move (not lift, mind you) were measured in ounces.

2. Use parentheses to enclose letters or numbers labeling items in a series.

> Regulations stipulated that only the following equipment could be used on the survival mission: (1) a knife, (2) thirty feet of parachute line, (3) a book of matches, (4) two ponchos, (5) an *E* tool, and (6) a signal flare.

3. Do not overuse parentheses.

Rough drafts are likely to contain more afterthoughts than necessary. As writers head into a sentence, they often think of additional details, occasionally working them in as best they can with parentheses. Usually such sentences should be revised so that the additional details no longer seem to be afterthoughts.

▶ Tucker's Restaurant serves homestyle breakfasts with fresh eggs,
warm

buttered toast, (which is still warm), sausage, bacon, waffles,

pancakes, and even kippers.

from ten to fifty million
▶ Researchers have said that ten million (estimates run as high as

fifty million) Americans have hypoglycemia.

P8-c Brackets

Use brackets to enclose any words or phrases that you have inserted into an otherwise word-for-word quotation.

> *Audubon* reports that "if there are not enough young to balance deaths, the end of the species [California condor] is inevitable."

The *Audubon* article did not contain the words *California condor* in the sentence quoted, since the context made clear what species was meant, so the writer in this example needed to add the name in brackets.

Brackets may also enclose material that substitutes for a word in the original source. The example would be just as correct without the word *species,* since the words *California condor* could substitute for it.

> *Audubon* reports that "if there are not enough young to balance deaths, the end of the [California condor] is inevitable."

The Latin word *sic* in brackets indicates that an error in a quoted sentence appears in the original source.

> According to the review, Suzanne Farrell's performance was brilliant, "exceding [*sic*] the expectations of even her most loyal fans."

Do not overuse *sic,* however, since calling attention to others' mistakes can appear snobbish. The quotation above, for example, might have been paraphrased instead: *According to the review, even Suzanne Farrell's most loyal fans were surprised by the brilliance of her performance.*

P8-d The ellipsis mark

The ellipsis mark consists of three spaced periods. Use an ellipsis mark to indicate that you have deleted material from an otherwise word-for-word quotation.

> Reuben reports that "when the amount of cholesterol circulating in the blood rises over . . . 300 milligrams per 100, the chances of a heart attack increase dramatically."

Do not ordinarily use the ellipsis mark at the beginning or at the end of a quotation. (See D2-b.)

P8-e The slash

Use the slash to separate two or three lines of poetry that have been run in with your text. Add a space both before and after the slash.

> In the opening lines of "Jordan," George Herbert pokes gentle fun at popular poems of his time: "Who says that fictions only and false hair / Become a verse? Is there in truth no beauty?"

More than three lines of poetry should be handled as block quotations set off from the text.

The slash may occasionally be used to separate options such as *pass/fail* and *producer/director.* Do not use a space before or after the slash.

> Roger Sommers, the play's producer/director, announced a change in casting.

Be sparing, however, in this use of the slash. In particular, avoid the use of *and/or, he/she,* and *his/her.*

M

Mechanics

M

Mechanics

M1

Capitalization

In addition to the following rules, a good dictionary can often tell you when to use capital letters.

M1-a Capitalize proper nouns and words derived from them; do not capitalize common nouns.

Proper nouns are the names of specific persons, places, and things. All other nouns are common nouns. The following types of words are usually capitalized: names for the deity, religions, religious followers, sacred books; words of family relationship used as names; particular places; nationalities and their languages, races, tribes; educational institutions, departments, degrees, particular courses; government departments, organizations, political parties; and historical movements, periods, events, documents.

PROPER NOUNS	COMMON NOUNS
God (used as a name)	a god
Book of Jeremiah	a book
Grandmother Bishop	my grandmother
Father (used as a name)	my father
Lake Superior	a picturesque lake
the Capital Center	a center for advanced studies
the South	a southern state
Japan, a Japanese garden	an ornamental garden
University of Wisconsin	a good university
Geology 101	geology
Environmental Protection Agency	a federal agency
Phi Kappa Psi	a fraternity
a Democrat	an independent
the Enlightenment	the eighteenth century
the Declaration of Independence	a treaty

Months, holidays, and days of the week are treated as proper nouns; the seasons and numbers of the days of the month are not.

Our academic year begins on a Tuesday in early September, right after Labor Day.

> My mother's birthday is in early summer, on the thirteenth of June.

Names of school subjects are capitalized only if they are names of languages. Names of particular courses are capitalized.

> This semester Austin is taking math, geography, geology, French, and English.

> Professor Anderson offers Modern American Fiction 501 to graduate students.

CAUTION: Do not capitalize common nouns to make them seem important. *Our company is currently hiring computer programmers* (not *Company, Computer Programmers*).

M1-b Capitalize titles of persons when used as part of a proper name but usually not when used alone.

> Prof. Margaret Barnes; Dr. Harold Stevens; John Scott Williams, Jr.; Anne Tilton, LL.D.

> District Attorney Marshall was reprimanded for badgering the witness.

> The district attorney was elected for a two-year term.

Usage varies when the title of an important public figure is used alone. *The president* (or *the President*) *vetoed the bill.*

M1-c Capitalize the first, last, and all major words in titles and subtitles of works such as books, articles, and songs.

In both titles and subtitles, major words — nouns, verbs, adjectives, and adverbs — should be capitalized. Minor words — articles, prepositions, and coordinating conjunctions — are not capitalized unless they are the first or last word of a title or subtitle. Capitalize the second part of a hyphenated term in a title if it is a major word but not if it is a minor word.

> *The Country of the Pointed Firs*
> *The Impossible Theater: A Manifesto*
> *The F-Plan Diet*

Capitalize chapter titles and the titles of other major divisions of a work following the same guidelines used for titles of complete works.

"Work and Play" in Santayana's *The Nature of Beauty*

M1-d Capitalize the first word of a sentence.

When lightning struck the house, the chimney collapsed.

Capitalize the first word in every line of poetry unless the poet uses a different convention.

When I consider everything that grows
Holds in perfection but a little moment   *—Shakespeare*

it was the week   that
i felt the city's narrow breezes rush about
me   *—Don L. Lee*

M1-e Capitalize the first word of a quoted sentence unless it is blended into the sentence that introduces it.

In *Time* magazine Robert Hughes writes, "There are only about sixty Watteau paintings on whose authenticity all experts agree."

Russell Baker has written that in our country "it is sport that is the opiate of the masses."

If a quoted sentence is interrupted by explanatory words, do not capitalize the first word after the interruption.

"If you wanted to go out," he said sharply, "you should have told me."

M1-f Do not capitalize the first word after a colon unless it begins an independent clause, in which case capitalization is optional.

Most of the bar's patrons can be divided into two groups: the occasional after-work socializers and the nothing-to-go-home-to regulars.

This we are forced to conclude: The [*or* the] federal government is needed to protect the rights of minorities.

M1-g Capitalize abbreviations for departments and agencies of government, other organizations, and corporations; capitalize trade names and the call letters of radio and television stations.

> EPA, FBI, OPEC, IBM, Xerox, WCRB, WWOR-TV

M2

Abbreviations

M2-a Abbreviate titles immediately before and after proper names.

TITLES BEFORE PROPER NAMES	TITLES AFTER PROPER NAMES
Mr. Ralph Meyer	William Albert, Sr.
Ms. Nancy Linehan	Thomas Hines, Jr.
Mrs. Edward Horn	Anita Lor, Ph.D.
Dr. Margaret Simmons	Robert Simkowski, M.D.
Rev. John Stone	William Lyons, M.A.
St. Joan of Arc	Margaret Chin, LL.D.
Prof. James Russo	Polly Stein, D.D.S.

Do not abbreviate a title if it is not used with a proper name.

> ▶ My history ~~prof.~~ *professor* was a specialist on America's use of the atomic
>
> bomb in World War II.

Avoid redundant titles such as *Dr. Susan Hassel, M.D.* Choose one title or the other: *Dr. Susan Hassel* or *Susan Hassel, M.D.*

M2-b Use commonly accepted abbreviations for the names of organizations, corporations, and countries.

Familiar abbreviations, often written without periods, are acceptable.

> CIA, FBI, AFL-CIO, NAACP, IBM, UPI, CBS,
> USA, USSR (or U.S.A., U.S.S.R.)

While in Washington the schoolchildren toured the FBI.

The YMCA has opened a new gym close to my office.

NOTE: When using an unfamiliar abbreviation (such as UAW for United Auto Workers) throughout a paper, write the full name followed by the abbreviation in parentheses at the first mention of the name. Then use the abbreviation throughout the rest of the paper.

M2-c Use the following commonly accepted abbreviations: B.C., A.D., A.M. (or a.m.), P.M. (or p.m.), $, No. (or no.).

40 B.C. (follows the date)	4:00 A.M.	$100
A.D. 44 (precedes the date)	6:00 P.M.	No. 12

NOTE: Use the abbreviations *No.* and *$* only with specific numbers and amounts. Otherwise, write out the words.

▶ There were an odd ~~no.~~ *number* of seats in the room.

M2-d Use commonly accepted Latin abbreviations sparingly.

Use commonly accepted Latin abbreviations in footnotes and bibliographies and in informal writing for comments in parentheses.

cf. (Latin *confer,* "compare")
e.g. (Latin *exempli gratia,* "for example")
et al. (Latin *et alii,* "and others")

etc. (Latin *et cetera,* "and so forth")
i.e. (Latin *id est,* "that is")
N.B. (Latin *nota bene,* "note well")

She hated the slice-and-dice genre of horror movies (e.g., *Happy Birthday to Me, Psycho, Friday the Thirteenth*).

Harold Simms et al., *The Race for Space*

In formal writing use the appropriate English phrases.

▶ Many obsolete laws remain on the books, ~~e.g.,~~ *for example* a law in Vermont

forbidding an unmarried man and woman to sit less than six

inches apart on a park bench.

M2-e Avoid inappropriate abbreviations.

In formal writing, the following abbreviations are not commonly accepted: personal names, units of measurement, days of the week, holidays, months, courses of study, divisions of written works, states and countries (except in addresses and except Washington, DC). Do not abbreviate *Company* and *Incorporated* unless their abbreviated forms are part of an official name.

PERSONAL NAME   Charles (not Chas.)

UNITS OF MEASUREMENT   pounds (not lb.)

DAYS OF THE WEEK   Monday through Friday (not Mon. through Fri.)

HOLIDAYS   Christmas (not Xmas)

MONTHS   January, February, March (not Jan., Feb., Mar.)

COURSES OF STUDY   political science, psychology (not poli. sci., psych.)

DIVISIONS OF WRITTEN WORKS   chapter, page (not ch., p.)

STATES AND COUNTRIES   Massachusetts, New York (not MA or Mass., NY)

PARTS OF A BUSINESS NAME   Adams Lighting Company (not Adams Lighting Co.); Fletcher and Brothers, Incorporated (not Fletcher and Bros., Inc.)

▶ Eliza promised to buy me one l̶b̶. *pound* of Godiva chocolate for my birthday, which was last F̶r̶i̶. *Friday.*

M3

Numbers

M3-a Spell out numbers of one or two words. Use figures for numbers that require more than two words to spell out.

▶ Now, some 8̶ *eight* years later, Muffin is still with us.

176

▶ I counted ~~one hundred seventy-six~~ records on the shelf.
                                    ∧

If a sentence begins with a number, spell out the number or rewrite the sentence.

One hundred fifty

▶ ~~150~~ children in our program need expensive dental treatment.
  ∧

Rewriting the sentence will also correct the error and may be less awkward if the number is long: *There are 150 children in our program who need expensive dental treatment.*

EXCEPTIONS: In technical and some business writing, figures are preferred even when spellings would be brief, but usage varies.

When several numbers appear in the same passage, many writers choose consistency rather than strict adherence to the rule.

When one number immediately follows another, spell out one and use figures for the other: three 100-meter events, 60 four-poster beds.

M3-b Generally, figures are acceptable for dates, addresses, percentages, fractions, decimals, scores, statistics and other numerical results, exact amounts of money, divisions of books and plays, pages, identification numbers, and the time.

DATES   July 4, 1776, 56 B.C., A.D. 30

ADDRESSES   77 Latches Lane, 519 West 42nd Street

PERCENTAGES   55 percent (or 55%)

FRACTIONS, DECIMALS   ½, 0.047

SCORES   7 to 3, 21–18

STATISTICS   average age 37, average weight 180

SURVEYS   4 out of 5

EXACT AMOUNTS OF MONEY $105.37, $106,000, $0.05

DIVISIONS OF BOOKS   volume 3, chapter 4, page 189

DIVISIONS OF PLAYS   Act III, scene iii (or Act 3, scene 3)

IDENTIFICATION NUMBERS   serial number 10988675

TIME OF DAY   4:00 P.M., 1:30 A.M.

▶ Several doctors put up ~~two hundred fifty-five thousand dollars~~ for

$255,000

the construction of a golf course.

▶ Though I was working on a ~~nineteen thirty-nine~~ sewing machine,

1939

my costume turned out well.

NOTE: When not using A.M. or P.M., write out the time in words (*four o'clock in the afternoon, twelve noon, seven in the morning*).

M4

Italics (underlining)

In handwritten or typed papers <u>underlining</u> represents *italics,* a slanting typeface used in printed material.

M4-a Underline the titles of books, plays, films, long poems, musical compositions, works of visual art, magazines, newspapers, and pamphlets.

TITLES OF BOOKS   *The Great Gatsby, David Copperfield*

PLAYS   *Julius Caesar, Death of a Salesman*

FILMS   *The French Connection, Star Wars*

LONG POEMS   T. S. Eliot's *The Waste Land,* Milton's *Paradise Lost*

MUSICAL COMPOSITIONS   Handel's *Messiah,* Gershwin's *Porgy and Bess*

WORKS OF VISUAL ART   Rodin's *The Thinker,* da Vinci's *The Last Supper*

MAGAZINES   *Time, Scientific American*

NEWSPAPERS   the *New York Times,* the *Boston Globe*

PAMPHLETS   Thomas Paine's *Common Sense*

The titles of other works, such as short stories, essays, songs, and short poems, are enclosed in quotation marks. (See P6-c.)

NOTE: Do not underline the Bible or the titles of books in the Bible (Genesis, not *Genesis*); the titles of legal documents (the Constitution, not the *Constitution*); or the titles of your own papers.

M4-b Underline the names of spacecraft, aircraft, ships, and trains.

Challenger, Spirit of St. Louis, Queen Elizabeth II, Silver Streak

▶ The success of the Soviet's <u>Sputnik</u> galvanized the U.S. space

program.

M4-c Underline foreign words in an English sentence.

▶ Although Joe's method seemed to be successful, I decided to

establish my own <u>modus operandi</u>.

EXCEPTION: Do not underline foreign words that have become part of the English language—"laissez-faire," "fait accompli," "habeas corpus," and "per diem," for example.

M4-d Underline words, letters, and numbers mentioned as themselves.

▶ Tim assured us that the howling probably came from his

bloodhound, Hill Billy, but his <u>probably</u> stuck in our minds.

▶ Sarah called her father by his given name, Johnny, but she was

unable to pronounce the <u>J.</u>

▶ A big <u>3</u> was painted on the door.

NOTE: Quotation marks may be used instead of underlining to set off words mentioned as words. (See P6-d.)

M4-e Avoid excessive underlining for emphasis.

Frequent underlining to emphasize words or ideas is distracting and should be used sparingly.

▶ Tennis is a sport that has become an ~~addiction~~.

M5

Spelling

You learned to spell from repeated experience with words in both reading and writing, but especially writing. Words have a look, a sound, and even a feel to them as the hand moves across the page. As you proofread, you can probably tell if a word doesn't look quite right. In such cases, the solution is obvious: Look up the word in the dictionary. (See W5.)

A word processor equipped with a spelling checker is a useful alternative to a dictionary, but only up to a point. A spelling checker will not tell you how to spell words not listed in its dictionary; nor will it help you catch words commonly confused, such as *accept* and *except,* or common typographical errors, such as *own* for *won.* For many words, you still need to turn to the dictionary.

M5-a Become familiar with the major spelling rules.

1. Use *i* before *e* except after *c* or when sounded like *ay,* as in *neighbor* and *weigh.*

I BEFORE E	relieve, believe, sieve, niece, fierce, frieze
E BEFORE I	receive, deceive, sleigh, freight, eight
EXCEPTIONS	seize, either, weird, height, foreign, leisure

2. Generally, drop a final silent *e* when adding a suffix that begins with a vowel. Keep the final *e* if the suffix begins with a consonant.

desire, desiring; remove, removable

achieve, achievement; care, careful

Words such as *changeable, judgment, argument,* and *truly* are exceptions.

3. When adding *-s* or *-ed* to words ending in *y*, ordinarily change *y* to *i* when the *y* is preceded by a consonant but not when it is preceded by a vowel.

comedy, comedies; dry, dried

monkey, monkeys; play, played

With proper names ending in *y*, however, do not change the *y* to *i* even if it is preceded by a consonant: *Dougherty, the Doughertys.*

4. If a final consonant is preceded by a single vowel *and* the consonant ends a one-syllable word or a stressed syllable, double the consonant when adding a suffix beginning with a vowel.

bet, betting; commit, committed; occur, occurrence

5. Add *-s* to form the plural of most nouns; add *-es* to singular nouns ending in *-s, -sh, -ch,* and *-x*.

table, tables; paper, papers

church, churches; dish, dishes

Ordinarily add *-s* to nouns ending in *-o* when the *o* is preceded by a vowel. Add *-es* when it is preceded by a consonant.

radio, radios; video, videos

hero, heroes; tomato, tomatoes

To form the plural of a hyphenated compound word, add the *-s* to the chief word even if it does not appear at the end.

mother-in-law, mothers-in-law

NOTE: English words derived from other languages such as Latin or French sometimes form the plural as they would in their original language.

medium, media; criterion, criteria; chateau, chateaux

M5-b Discriminate between words that sound alike but have different meanings.

Pronunciation can be a useful guide to spelling, but don't rely too heavily on it. As you know by now, words are not always spelled as they sound, especially in English. Think of the different sounds for *-ough* in the following words: *rough, thorough, through, slough.* Other sets of words that cause spelling troubles are homophones, words that sound alike but have different meanings and spellings.

HOMOPHONES (WORDS WITH SIMILAR PRONUNCIATION
AND DIFFERENT MEANINGS)
accept (to receive)
except (to take or leave out)

affect (v., to exert an influence)
effect (v., to accomplish; n., result)

ascent (a climb)
assent (agreement)

brake (something used to stop movement)
break (to split or smash into pieces)

capital (seat of government; material wealth)
capitol (building in which a legislative body meets)

cite (to quote)
sight (vision)
site (position, place)

coarse (of ordinary or inferior quality)
course (path, policy chosen)

complement (something that completes)
compliment (praise)

desert (v., to withdraw from)
dessert (sweet course at the end of a meal)

discreet (prudent, tactful)
discrete (constituting a separate entity)

elicit (to draw or bring out)
illicit (illegal)

eminent (famous, respected)
immanent (indwelling, inherent)
imminent (ready to take place)

formally (in a customary manner)
formerly (in time past)

hole (hollow place)
whole (entire, unhurt)

its (of or belonging to it)
it's (contraction for *it is*)

lead (n., a metal)
led (past tense of the verb *lead*)

loose (free, not securely attached)
lose (to fail to keep, to be deprived of)

manner (way)
manor (house)

pair (set of two)
pare (to prepare, trim)
pear (a fruit)

passed (past tense of the verb *pass*)
past (belonging to a former time)

principal (most important; a person who has authority)
principle (a general or fundamental truth)

rain (water falling in drops)
reign (to rule)
rein (restraining influence)

raise (to lift)
raze (to destroy, to lay level with the ground)

stationary (standing still)
stationery (writing paper)

straight (free from curves, bends, or angles)
strait (narrow space or passage)

than (conj., used to compare)
then (adverb of time)

their (belonging to them)
they're (contraction of *they are*)
there (that place or position)

to (prep., toward)
too (also, excessively)
two (one more than one in number)

weather (state of the atmosphere)
whether (indicating a choice between alternatives)

who's (contraction of *who is*)
whose (possessive of *who*)

your (possessive of *you*)
you're (contraction of *you are*)

M5-c Be alert to the following commonly misspelled words.

absence	Britain	disappoint	infinite
academic	bureau	disastrous	intelligence
accidentally	business	dissatisfied	interesting
accommodate	cafeteria	eighth	irrelevant
accomplish	calendar	eligible	irresistible
accumulate	candidate	eliminate	knowledge
achievement	category	embarrass	laboratory
acknowledge	cemetery	eminent	legitimate
acquaintance	changeable	emphasize	license
acquire	changing	entirely	lightning
across	characteristic	entrance	literature
address	chosen	environment	loneliness
aggravate	column	equivalent	maintenance
all right	coming	especially	maneuver
almost	commitment	exaggerated	marriage
although	committed	exhaust	mathematics
altogether	committee	existence	mischievous
always	comparative	experience	necessary
amateur	competitive	explanation	nevertheless
among	conceivable	extraordinary	noticeable
analyze	conference	extremely	obstacle
annual	conferred	familiar	occasion
answer	conqueror	fascinate	occasionally
apology	conscience	February	occur
apparently	conscientious	foreign	occurred
appearance	conscious	forty	occurrence
appropriate	convenient	fourth	optimistic
arctic	courteous	friend	original
argument	criticism	government	outrageous
arising	criticize	grammar	pamphlet
arithmetic	curiosity	guard	parallel
arrangement	dealt	guidance	particularly
ascend	decision	harass	pastime
association	definitely	height	perform
athlete	descendant	humorous	performance
athletics	describe	illiterate	permissible
attendance	description	imaginary	perseverance
audience	despair	imagination	perspiration
bachelor	desperate	immediately	phenomenon
basically	develop	incidentally	physically
beginning	dictionary	incredible	picnicking
believe	dining	indefinitely	playwright
benefited	disagree	indispensable	politics
brilliant	disappear	inevitable	practically

precede	quite	schedule	thorough
precedence	quizzes	secretary	tragedy
preference	receive	seize	transferred
preferred	recognize	separate	tries
prejudice	recommend	sergeant	truly
preparation	reference	several	Tuesday
prevalent	referred	similar	unanimous
primitive	regard	sincerely	unnecessarily
privilege	religion	soliloquy	until
probably	repetition	sophomore	usually
proceed	restaurant	specimen	vacuum
professor	rhythm	strictly	vengeance
prominent	rhythmical	subtly	villain
pronunciation	ridiculous	succeed	weird
quantity	roommate	surprise	whether
quiet	sandwich	temperature	writing

M6

The hyphen

M6-a Consult the dictionary to determine how to treat a compound word.

The dictionary will tell you whether to treat a compound word as a hyphenated compound (*water-repellent*), one word (*waterproof*), or two words (*water table*). If the compound word is not in the dictionary, treat it as two words.

▶ The prosecutor chose not to cross_examine any witnesses.
∧

▶ Grandma kept a small note book in her apron pocket.

▶ Alice walked through the looking-glass into a backward world.
/

M6-b Use a hyphen to connect two or more words functioning together as an adjective before a noun.

▶ Mrs. Douglas gave Mary a seashell and some newspaper_wrapped

fish to take home to her mother.
∧

Priscilla Hobbes is not yet a well‸known candidate.

Newspaper-wrapped and *well-known* are adjectives used before the nouns *fish* and *candidate*.

Generally, do not use a hyphen when such compounds follow the noun.

▶ After our television campaign, Priscilla Hobbes will be well/known.

Do not use a hyphen to connect *-ly* adverbs to the words they modify.

▶ A slowly/moving truck tied up traffic.

NOTE: In a series, hyphens are suspended.

Do you prefer first-, second-, or third-class tickets?

M6-c Hyphenate the written form of fractions and of compound numbers from twenty-one to ninety-nine.

▶ One‸fourth of my income goes to pay off the national debt.

M6-d Use the hyphen with the prefixes *all-*, *ex-*, and *self-* and with the suffix *-elect*.

▶ The charity is funneling more money into self‸help projects.

▶ Anne King is our club's president‸elect.

M6-e The hyphen is used in some words to avoid ambiguity or to separate awkward double or triple letters.

Without the hyphen there would be no way to distinguish between words such as *re-creation* and *recreation*.

Bicycling in the country is my favorite recreation.

The film was praised for its astonishing re-creation of nineteenth-century London.

Hyphens are sometimes used to separate awkward double or triple letters in compound words (*anti-intellectual, cross-stitch*). Check a dictionary for the standard form of the word.

M6-f If a word must be divided at the end of a line, divide it correctly.

1. Divide words between syllables.

▶ When I returned from overseas, I didn't ~~reco-~~ *recog-*
~~gnize~~ *nize* one face on the magazine covers.

2. Never divide one-syllable words.

▶ He didn't have the courage or the ~~stren-~~ *strength*
~~gth~~ to open the door.

3. Never divide a word so that a single letter stands alone at the end of a line or fewer than three letters begin a line.

▶ She'll bring her brother with her when she comes ~~a-~~
~~gain.~~ *again.*

▶ As audience to *The Mousetrap*, Hamlet is a ~~watch-~~
~~er~~ *watcher* watching watchers.

4. When dividing a compound word at the end of a line, either make the break between the words that form the compound or put the whole word on the next line.

▶ My niece is determined to become a long-~~dis-~~
~~tance~~ *distance* runner when she grows up.

M7

Manuscript formats

Specific manuscript formats are used in the business world for documents such as letters, résumés, memos, reports, and proposals. In the academic world you may need to learn manuscript conventions for essays, lab reports, case studies, and so on.

Standard formats for college essays, business letters, and résumés are described in this section. To learn how to format other types of writing, check with your professor or employer.

M7-a College essays

Professors have certain expectations about how a college essay should look. If your instructor provides formal guidelines, follow them; otherwise, use a standard essay format.

Materials

For a typed essay use $8\frac{1}{2}'' \times 11''$, 20-pound typing paper, not onionskin. Some instructors allow erasable or corrasable bond, but ink smears easily on this coated paper, so you should probably avoid it. Use a fresh typewriter ribbon, and if necessary clean the typewriter keys before you begin. A self-correcting typewriter will allow you to eliminate errors completely, but if you don't have access to such a typewriter, use Liquid Paper or some other white correction fluid. Some instructors will accept a line through a mistake with the correction neatly written or typed above. Use a caret ($\wedge$) to indicate where the correction should be inserted.

For an essay typed on a word processor, make sure that the print quality and the paper quality meet your instructor's standards. If the paper emerges from the printer in a continuous sheet, separate the pages, remove the feeder strips from the sides of the paper, and assemble the pages in order.

Before you consider submitting a handwritten essay, be sure that your instructor will accept work that is not typewritten. Use $8\frac{1}{2}'' \times 11''$, wide-ruled white paper, and write in blue or black ink on one side of the paper only. Do not use legal-size paper or sheets torn from a notebook. Obviously you should make your handwriting as clear as possible; if your handwriting is difficult to read, make an effort to type the essay or have it typed.

Title and identification

College essays normally do not require a separate title page. Unless instructed otherwise, against the left margin about one inch from the top of the paper, place your name, the instructor's name, the course name and number, and the date on separate lines. Double-space between lines.

Double-space after the heading and center the title of the essay in the width of the page. Capitalize the first and last words of the title and all other words except articles, prepositions, and coordinating conjunctions (see M1-c). If there is a subtitle, separate it from the title with a colon and follow the capitalization rules for titles. Do not underline your title or put it in quotation marks, and do not use a period after it.

If you decide to use a title page, center the title and all elements of identification. Place the title about one-third down the page. About an inch below the title, write "By" followed by your name. About an inch below your name on separate lines, write the course name and number, your instructor's name, and the date; double-space between lines.

Margins, spacing, and indentation

Leave margins of at least one inch but no more than an inch and a half at the top, bottom, and sides of the page.

Double-space between lines in a typewritten essay and indent the first line of each paragraph five spaces from the left margin.

For quotations of longer than four typed lines of prose or longer than three lines of verse, indent each line ten spaces from the left margin. Double-space between the body of the paper and the quotation, and double-space the lines of the quotation.

Pagination

Number all pages at the upper right corner, one-half inch below the top edge. (If you have a separate title page, the title page is uncounted and unnumbered.) Use arabic numerals (1, 2, 3, and so on). Do not put a period after the number and do not enclose the number in parentheses.

Punctuation and typing

In typing the essay, leave one space after words, commas, and semicolons and between the dots in ellipses. Leave two spaces after periods, question marks, and exclamation points. Usage is divided concerning spacing after a colon. Many authorities recommend two spaces, but the 1988 *MLA Handbook for Writers of Research Papers* (3rd edition) recommends one space.

To form a dash, type two hyphens with no space between them. Do not put a space either side of a dash.

Documentation

If in your essay you draw on written sources, you will need to document those sources according to a consistent system. See Documentation (D1–D5) for a survey of three commonly used systems.

Proofreading

Misspelled words, incorrect hyphenation, and errors in grammar and punctuation detract from the overall effect of an essay; if there are too many of these errors, readers will lose patience. Your ideas deserve clear and correct expression. Proofread the final draft of the essay and then proofread it again.

M7-b Business letters

In writing a business letter be direct, clear, and courteous, but do not hesitate to be firm if the situation calls for it. State your purpose or request at the beginning of the letter and include only pertinent information in the body. Follow conventions of form and usage, and avoid spelling errors.

Business letters usually follow one of three patterns: full block, block, and semiblock. In full block form, letterhead stationery, giving the return address of the writer (or of the writer's company), is used. Every element of the letter (including date, inside address, salutation, body, close, and signature) is typed flush with the left margin. In block form, the return address of the writer, the close, and the signature are moved to the right. Paragraphs are not indented but begin flush with the left margin. In semiblock form, considered the least formal of the three patterns, the return address, close, and signature are moved to the right, and the beginning of each paragraph is indented five spaces from the left margin.

Type business letters on letterhead stationery or on unlined paper that is at least 5½″ × 8½″ (8½″ × 11″ is standard). Type on only one side of the paper, single-spacing the body of the letter and

Return address — ⌈ 14 Closter Road
                   Langdon, ND 58249
                 ⌊ March 12, 1989

Personnel Manager   ⌉
Minnesota Public Radio   ├— Inside
45 East 8th Street   │   address
St. Paul, MN 55101   ⌋

Dear Sir or Madam: —⊐— Salutation

I am applying for the summer internship you listed
with the Job Information and Placement Center at
North Dakota State University. I am currently a
sophomore at North Dakota State University, with a
major in mass communication and a minor in English.

As the enclosed résumé shows, I have had a variety
of experiences in radio. In addition to producing
the weekly debate show "The Forum" for the university
radio station, KDSU, I have also taken several upper-   Body
level courses in broadcast journalism and audio production. My job last summer at KDSU provided an
overview of the administrative aspects of radio, and
I believe the internship you offer will give me an
opportunity to acquire specific experience in the
production area of broadcasting.

I would be happy to send you a transcript of "The
Forum." I am available for an interview almost
anytime and can be reached at (701) 256-7011.

I look forward to hearing from you.

Close ——⊐Sincerely,

Signature —⌈ *Barbara C. Hansen*
           ⌊ Barbara C. Hansen

Enc.

double-spacing between paragraphs. The sample letter on the next page, in block form, illustrates the proper placement of each part of a business letter. The return address is followed by the date. (Note that the writer's name is not part of this heading.) The inside address includes the full name, title, and complete address of the person to whom the letter is written. (This information is repeated as the address on the envelope.) The inside address is typed flush left, a few lines below the return address heading. The salutation, or greeting, is typed two lines below the inside address. A colon follows the salutation, and the body of the letter begins two lines below the greeting.

In the salutation use *Ms.* if you are writing to a woman whose title or marital status you do not know or if the woman prefers this form of address. If you are not writing to a particular person, you can use the salutation *Dear Sir or Madam* or you can address the company itself—*Dear Solar Technology.*

In block form the close is lined up with the return address and typed two lines below the end of the letter. Common closes are *Yours truly, Very truly yours,* and *Sincerely.* (Note that only the first word of the close is capitalized.) The name of the writer is typed four lines below the close, leaving room for the written signature between the close and the typed name. The name of the writer should not be prefaced by a title or followed by an abbreviation for a title or position. This information can be included in a separate line under the typed name (for example, *Director* or *Sales Manager*).

Other information can be included below the signature and flush with the left margin (for example: *Enc.,* indicating that something is enclosed with the letter; *cc: Mr. Theodore Jones,* indicating that a copy of the letter is being sent to Mr. Jones, a third party; or *JEF:njl,* indicating that JEF [the writer's initials] wrote the letter and njl typed it).

The name and return address of the writer is typed in the upper left-hand corner of the envelope. The addressee's name, title, and complete address are typed just right of the center of the envelope. The letter (which should be about the same width as the envelope) is folded in thirds.

M7-c Résumés

An effective résumé presents relevant information in a clear and concise form. Every résumé should include name, address, and telephone number; a history of education and employment; a list of special interests or related activities; and information about how to

RÉSUMÉ

Barbara C. Hansen
14 Closter Road
Langdon, ND 58249
(701) 256-7011

Position Desired   Internship in News Department

Education
1987 to present   North Dakota State University,
                         Fargo, ND. B.A. in mass communi-
                         cation expected May 1991. Minor
                         in English.

1983-1987   Langdon High School, Langdon, ND.

Experience
1987 to present   Producer of "The Forum," a weekly
                         broadcast on KDSU, the university
                         radio station. Responsibilities
                         include selecting the issues and
                         the participants, moderating the
                         debates.

May-Sept. 1988   Receptionist, KNDK radio station,
                         Langdon, ND. Answered telephones;
                         performed various clerical duties.

Related Interests   Volunteer tutoring in the Moorhead
and Activities   area public schools; basketball;
                         reading.

References   Academic references available
                         from the Job Information and
                         Placement Office at North Dakota
                         State University, Fargo, ND
                         58105.

                         Employment   Ms. Kimberly Quinlan
                         Reference   KNDK
                                      Langdon, ND 58249

                         Personal   Mr. Stephen Hurley
                         Reference   45 Main Street
                                      Langdon, ND 58249

obtain references. You may also include personal information such as date of birth or marital status, but such information is not necessary. Some résumés name the specific position desired. If you are applying for a number of different positions, you may find it more useful to name a broader employment goal.

In the education history, begin with the institution you are currently attending and work backward to your high school, listing degrees and dates of attendance. If you have won special honors, include them. In the employment history, list your most recent job first and work backward. Give the dates of employment and the company names and addresses. You can also list your supervisors. Describe your responsibilities, highlighting those tasks or skills related to the position you are seeking. In listing special interests, concentrate on those related to your employment goal. Instead of listing the names and addresses of references, you can state that references are available on request.

In a résumé, present yourself in the best possible light, but do not distort any of the facts about your experience or qualifications. Select details wisely and your résumé will be a valuable tool.

When you send your résumé, you should include a letter that tells what position you seek and where you learned about it. The letter should also summarize your education and past experience, relating them to the job you are applying for. You may want to highlight a specific qualification and refer the reader to your résumé for more information. End the letter with a suggestion for a meeting, and tell your prospective employer when you will be available.

Documentation

D

Documentation

In academic research papers and in any other writing that borrows information from sources, the borrowed information — quotations, summaries, paraphrases, and any facts or ideas that are not common knowledge — must be clearly documented.

Traditionally, documentation took the form of footnotes or endnotes (see D5), but many academic disciplines now use a system of parenthetical references in the text of the paper (known as *in-text citations*). These in-text citations refer readers to a list of works cited at the end of the paper.

The system of in-text citations used in English and the humanities, recommended by the Modern Language Association (MLA), is described in D3; the system used in the social sciences, recommended by the American Psychological Association (APA), is described in D4.

D1

When to cite a source; avoiding plagiarism

In research writing, sources are cited for two reasons: to alert readers to the sources of your information and to give credit to the writers from whom you have borrowed words and ideas. To borrow another writer's words and ideas without proper acknowledgment is a form of dishonesty known as plagiarism.

To avoid plagiarism, you must cite all quotations, summaries, and paraphrases as well as any facts or ideas that are not common knowledge. In addition, you must be careful to put paraphrases and summaries in your own words.

D1-a Cite all quotations.

Quotations must be copied accurately, word-for-word, and they must be placed in quotation marks unless they have been formally set off from the rest of the text (see D2-c). The following example and other examples in this section are documented with the MLA style of in-text citation (see D3).

> According to Eugene Linden, "There is a good deal of evidence that maternal behavior in chimps is not entirely automatic" (93-94).

D1-b Cite summaries, paraphrases, and any facts or ideas that are not common knowledge.

A summary condenses information from a source, perhaps capsulizing a chapter in a short paragraph or a paragraph in a single sentence. A paraphrase reports information in roughly the same number of words used by the source. Neither a summary nor a paraphrase borrows extensive language from a source. (See D1-c.)

ORIGINAL SOURCE

Public and scientific interest in the question of apes' ability to use language first soared some 15 years ago when Washoe, a chimpanzee raised like a human child by R. Allen Gardner and Beatrice Gardner of the University of Nevada, learned to make hand signs for many words and even seemed to be making short sentences.   —Erik Eckholm

SUMMARY

Interest in the ability of apes to use language was sparked in the early seventies, when a chimpanzee named Washoe was taught sign language by R. Allen Gardner and Beatrice Gardner (Eckholm B7).

PARAPHRASE

Interest in the ability of apes to learn language mounted in the early seventies, with reports that Washoe, a chimpanzee raised and trained by professors R. Allen Gardner and Beatrice Gardner, had learned words in sign language and may even have created short sentences (Eckholm B7).

In addition to citing summaries and paraphrases, cite any other specific borrowings from a source: statistics, little-known facts, controversial data, charts, graphs, diagrams, and original ideas. The only exception is common knowledge—information that readers could find in any number of general sources because it is commonly known. For example, the current population of the United States is common knowledge as are the dates of the Civil War and the names of the men who first landed on the moon.

As a rule, when you have seen certain facts repeatedly in your reading, you don't need to cite them. When they have appeared in only one or two sources or when they are controversial, however, you should cite them. When in doubt, cite the source.

D1-c Put summaries and paraphrases in your own words.

When you summarize or paraphrase, it is not enough to name the source; you must restate the source's meaning using only your own words. You are guilty of plagiarism, a form of academic dishonesty, if you half copy the author's sentences — either by mixing the author's well-chosen words without using quotation marks or by plugging your own synonyms into the author's sentence structure. The following paraphrases are plagiarized — even though the source is cited — because their language is too close to that of the original source.

ORIGINAL VERSION
If the existence of a signing ape was unsettling for linguists, it was also startling news for animal behaviorists.

UNACCEPTABLE BORROWING OF WORDS
An ape who knew sign language unsettled linguists and startled animal behaviorists (Davis 26).

UNACCEPTABLE BORROWING OF STRUCTURE
If the presence of a sign-language-using chimp was disturbing for scientists studying language, it was also surprising to scientists studying animal behavior (Davis 26).

To avoid plagiarizing an author's wording, resist the temptation to look at the source while you are summarizing or paraphrasing. Close the book, write from memory, and then open the book to check for accuracy. This technique prevents you from being captivated by the words on the page.

ACCEPTABLE PARAPHRASE
When they learned of an ape's ability to use sign language, both linguists and animal behaviorists were taken by surprise (Davis 26).

D2

How to integrate quotations

Readers should be able to move from your own words to the words you quote from a source without feeling a jolt.

D2-a Use signal phrases.

Avoid dropping quotations into the text without warning; instead, provide clear signal phrases, usually including the author's name, to prepare readers for the source.

> **DROPPED QUOTATION**
>
> Although the bald eagle is still listed as an endan-
> gered species, its ever-increasing population is very
> encouraging.   "The bald eagle seems to have stabi-
> lized its population, at the very least, almost
> everywhere" (Sheppard 96).

> **QUOTATION WITH SIGNAL PHRASE**
>
> Although the bald eagle is still listed as an endan-
> gered species, its ever-increasing population is very
> encouraging.   <u>According to ornithologist Jay Sheppard</u>,
> "The bald eagle seems to have stabilized its popula-
> tion, at the very least, almost everywhere" (96).

NOTE: The preceding example and other examples in this section are documented with the MLA style of in-text citation (see D3).

To avoid monotony, try to vary your signal phrases. The following models suggest a range of possibilities.

> In the words of researcher Herbert Terrace, "..."
>
> As Flora Davis has noted, "..."
>
> The Gardners, Washoe's trainers, point out that "..."
>
> "...," claims linguist Noam Chomsky.

Psychologist H. S. Terrace offers an odd argument for this view: ". . ."

Terrace answers these objections with the following analysis: ". . ."

When the signal phrase includes a verb, choose one that is appropriate in the context. Is your source arguing a point, making an observation, reporting a fact, drawing a conclusion, refuting an argument, or stating a belief? By choosing an appropriate verb, such as one on the following list, you can make your source's stance clear.

acknowledges	comments	endorses	reasons
adds	compares	grants	refutes
admits	confirms	illustrates	rejects
agrees	contends	implies	reports
argues	declares	insists	responds
asserts	denies	notes	suggests
believes	disputes	observes	thinks
claims	emphasizes	points out	writes

It is not always necessary to quote full sentences from a source. At times you may wish to borrow only a phrase or to weave part of a source's sentence into your own sentence structure:

> Brian Millsap claims that the banning of DDT in 1972 was "the major turning point" leading to the eagles' comeback (2).

> The ultrasonography machine takes approximately 250 views of each breast, step by step. Mary Spletter likens the process to "examining an entire loaf of bread, one slice at a time" (40).

D2-b Learn to use the ellipsis mark and brackets.

Two useful marks of punctuation, the ellipsis mark and brackets, allow you to keep quoted material to a minimum and to integrate it smoothly into your text.

The ellipsis mark

To condense a quoted passage, you can use the ellipsis mark (three periods, with spaces between) to indicate that you have omitted words. The words that remain must be grammatically complete.

```
In a recent New York Times article, Erik Eckholm re-
ports that "a 4-year-old pygmy chimpanzee . . . has
demonstrated what scientists say are the most human-
like linguistic skills ever documented in another
animal" (A1).
```

The writer has omitted the words *at a research center near Atlanta,* which appeared in the original.

When you want to omit a full sentence or more, use a period before the three ellipsis dots.

```
According to Wade, the horse Clever Hans "could appar-
ently count by tapping out numbers with his hoof. . . .
Clever Hans owes his celebrity to his master's inno-
cence.  Von Osten sincerely believed he had taught
Hans to solve arithmetical problems" (1349).
```

Ordinarily, do not use an ellipsis mark at the beginning or at the end of a quotation. Your readers will understand that the quoted material is taken from a longer passage. The only exception occurs when you have omitted words at the end of the final quoted sentence.

Obviously you should not use an ellipsis mark to distort the meaning of your source.

Brackets

Brackets (square parentheses) allow you to insert words of your own into quoted material, perhaps to explain a confusing reference or to keep a sentence grammatical in your context.

```
Robert Seyfarth reports that "Premack [a scientist at
the University of Pennsylvania] taught a seven-year-
old chimpanzee, Sarah, that the word for 'apple' was a
small, plastic triangle" (13).
```

If your typewriter has no brackets, ink them in by hand.

D2-c Set off long quotations.

When you quote more than four typed lines of prose, set off the quotation by indenting it ten spaces from the left margin. Use the normal right margin and do not single-space.

Long quotations should be introduced by an informative sentence, usually followed by a colon. Quotation marks are unnecessary because the indented format tells readers that the words are taken directly from the source.

```
Desmond describes how Washoe, when the Gardners re-
turned her to an ape colony in Oklahoma, tried signing
to the other apes:
          One particularly memorable day, a snake
          spread terror through the castaways on the
          ape island, and all but one fled in panic.
          This male sat absorbed, staring intently at
          the serpent.  Then Washoe was seen running
          over signing to him "come, hurry up." (42)
```

Notice that in the MLA style of citation, the parenthetical citation at the end of an indented quotation goes outside the final period.

D3

MLA style

The Modern Language Association (MLA) recommends in-text citations that refer the reader to a list of works cited.

D3-a MLA in-text citations

The Modern Language Association's in-text citations are made with a combination of signal phrases and parenthetical references. A signal phrase indicates that something taken from a source (such as a quotation, summary, or paraphrase) is about to be used; usually the signal phrase includes the author's name. The parenthetical reference includes at least a page number.

Citations in parentheses should be as concise as possible but complete enough so that readers can find the source in the list of works cited at the end of the paper, where works are listed alphabetically under the author's last name. The following models illustrate the form for the MLA style of citation.

AUTHOR IN SIGNAL PHRASE, PAGE NUMBER IN PARENTHESES Ordinarily, you should introduce the material being cited with a signal phrase that includes the author's name. In addition to preparing readers for the source, the signal phrase allows you to keep the citation within the parentheses brief.

> Flora Davis reports that a chimp at the Yerkes Primate
> Research Center "has combined words into new sentences
> that she was never taught" (67).

The signal phrase — "Flora Davis reports" — provides the name of the author; the parenthetical citation gives the page number where the quoted sentence may be found. By looking up the author's last name in the list of works cited, readers will find complete information about the work's title, publisher, and date of publication.

AUTHOR AND PAGE NUMBER IN PARENTHESES If the signal phrase does not include the author's name (or if there is no signal phrase), the author's last name must appear in parentheses along with the page number.

> Although the baby chimp lived only a few hours, Washoe
> signed to it before it died (Davis 42).

WHEN TO INCLUDE A TITLE Ordinarily the title of the work does not need to be included in either the signal phrase or the parentheses. However, if your paper cites two or more works by the same author (or by authors with the same last name), either mention the title in the signal phrase or use a short form of the title in parentheses.

> In <u>Eloquent Animals</u>, Flora Davis reports that a chimp
> at the Yerkes Primate Research Center "has combined
> words into new sentences that she was never taught"
> (67).

> Flora Davis reports that a chimp at the Yerkes Primate
> Research Center "has combined words into new sentences
> that she was never taught" (<u>Eloquent</u> 67).

In the rare case when both the author and a short title must be given in parentheses, the citation should appear as in this example:

> Although the baby chimpanzee lived only for a few

hours, Washoe signed to it before it died (Davis,

Eloquent 42).

A WORK WITH TWO OR MORE AUTHORS   If your source has two or three authors, name them in the signal phrase or include them in the parenthetical reference.

Patterson and Linden agree that the gorilla Koko ac-

quired language more slowly than a normal speaking

child (83-90).

If your source has more than three authors, include only the first author's name followed by "et al." (Latin for "and others") in the signal phrase or in the parenthetical reference.

The study was extended for two years, and only after

results were duplicated on both coasts did the authors

publish their results (Doe et al. 137).

CORPORATE AUTHOR   Either name the corporate author in the signal phrase or include a shortened version in the parentheses.

The Internal Revenue Service warns businesses that

deductions for "lavish and extravagant entertainment"

are not allowed (43).

UNKNOWN AUTHOR   If the author is not given, either use the complete title in a signal phrase or use a short form of the title in the parentheses.

The UFO reported by the crew of a Japan Air Lines

flight remains a mystery. Radar tapes did not confirm

the presence of another craft ("Strange Encounter" 26).

A MULTIVOLUME WORK   If your paper cites more than one volume of a multivolume work, you must indicate in the parentheses which volume you are referring to.

Terman's studies of gifted children reveal a pattern

of accelerated language acquisition (2: 279).

If your paper cites only one volume of a multivolume work, the volume number will be mentioned in the list of works cited at the end of the paper. You do not need to include it in the parentheses.

A NOVEL, A PLAY, OR A POEM In citing literary sources, include information that will enable readers to find the passage in various editions of the work. For a novel, put the page number first and then indicate the part or chapter in which the passage can be found.

> Fitzgerald's narrator captures Gatsby in a moment of
> isolation: "A sudden emptiness seemed to flow now from
> the windows and the great doors, endowing with com-
> plete isolation the figure of the host" (56; ch. 3).

For a verse play, list the act, scene, and line numbers. Use arabic numerals unless your instructor prefers roman numerals.

> In his famous advice to the players, Hamlet defines
> the purpose of theater, "whose end, both at the first
> and now, was and is, to hold, as 'twere, the mirror up
> to nature" (3.2.21-23).

For a poem, cite the part (if there are a number of parts) and the line numbers.

> When Homer's Odysseus came to the hall of Circe, he
> found his men "mild / in her soft spell, fed on her
> drug of evil" (10.209-11).

A WORK IN AN ANTHOLOGY A work in an anthology will be listed in the works cited under the name of the author of the work, not the editor of the anthology. In the citation, put the name of the author of the work in the signal phrase or in the parentheses.

> At the end of Kate Chopin's "The Story of an Hour,"
> Mrs. Mallard drops dead upon learning that her husband
> is alive. In the final irony of the story, doctors
> report that she has died of a "joy that kills" (25).

INDIRECT SOURCE When a writer's or speaker's quoted words appear in a source written by someone else, begin the citation with the abbreviation "qtd. in."

> "We only used seven signs in his presence," says
> Fouts. "All of his signs were learned from the other
> chimps at the laboratory" (qtd. in Toner 24).

PARENTHETICAL CITATION OF TWO OR MORE WORKS You may want to cite more than one source to document a particular point. Separate the citations with a semicolon.

> With intensive training, the apes in this study
>
> learned more than 200 signs or signals (Desmond 229;
>
> Linden 173).

Multiple citations can be distracting to readers, however, so the technique should not be overused. If you want to alert your reader to several sources that discuss a particular topic, consider using a note instead (discussed next).

Using footnotes or endnotes with parenthetical documentation

Researchers who use the MLA system of parenthetical documentation may also use footnotes or endnotes for one of two purposes:

1. to provide additional information that might interrupt the flow of the paper yet is important enough to include;
2. to refer readers to sources not included in the list of works cited.

Footnotes appear at the foot of the page; endnotes appear at the end of the paper, just before the list of works cited. For either style, the notes are numbered consecutively throughout the paper. The text of the paper contains a raised arabic numeral that corresponds to the number of the note.

TEXT

> The apes' achievements cannot be explained away as the
>
> simple results of conditioning or unconscious cueing
>
> by trainers.[1]

NOTE

> [1] For a discussion of the cueing of animals, see
>
> Wade 1349-51.

Notes used with parenthetical documentation (for the special purposes mentioned in this section) should not be confused with notes used as an alternative to parenthetical documentation. (See D5.)

D3-b MLA list of works cited

A list of works cited, which appears at the end of your paper, gives full publishing information for each of the sources you have cited in the paper. Start on a new page and title your list "Works Cited." Then list in alphabetical order all the sources that you have cited in the paper. Unless your instructor asks for them, sources not actually cited in the paper should not be given in this list, even if you may have read them. Alphabetize the list by the last name of the author (or editor); if there is no author or editor, alphabetize by the first word of the title other than *a, an,* or *the*.

Do not indent the first line of entries in the list of works cited but indent any additional lines. This technique highlights the names by which the list has been alphabetized.

The following models illustrate the form that the Modern Language Association (MLA) recommends for works cited entries.

BASIC FORMAT FOR A BOOK For most books, arrange the information into three units, each followed by a period: (1) the author's name, last name first; (2) the title and subtitle, underlined; and (3) the place of publication, the publisher, and the date.

```
Davis, Flora.  Eloquent Animals: A Study in Animal

    Communication.  New York: Coward, 1978.
```

The information is taken from the title page of the book and from the reverse side of the title page (the copyright page), not from the outside cover. The complete name of the publisher (in this case Coward, McCann & Geoghegan, Inc.) need not be given. You may use a short form as long as it is easily identifiable; omit terms such as *Press, Inc.,* and *Co.* except when naming university presses such as Harvard University Press. The date to use in your bibliographic entry is the latest copyright date.

TWO OR MORE AUTHORS Name the authors in the order in which they are presented on the title page; reverse the name of only the first author.

```
Fisher, Roger, and William Ury.  Getting to Yes:

    Negotiating Agreement without Giving In.

    Boston: Houghton, 1981.
```

The names of three authors are separated by commas: Smith, Margaret, Sharon Jones, and Harry Brown. For four or more authors, cite only the first one, followed by "et al." (the Latin abbreviation for "and others"): Doe, Jane, et al. The procedure for citing multiple authors of periodical articles is the same as for citing multiple authors of books.

EDITORS An entry for an editor is similar to that for an author except that the name is followed by a comma and the abbreviation "ed." for "editor." If there is more than one editor, use the abbreviation "eds." (for "editors").

Lenneberg, Eric H., and Elizabeth Lenneberg, eds.

  Foundations of Language Development. New York:

  Academic, 1975.

AUTHOR WITH AN EDITOR Begin with the author and title, followed by the name of the editor. In this case the abbreviation "Ed." means "edited by," so it is the same for one or multiple editors.

Shakespeare, William. The Tragedy of Macbeth.

  Ed. Louis B. Wright and Virginia A. Lamar.

  New York: Washington Square, 1959.

TRANSLATION List the entry under the name of the author, not the translator. After the title, write "Trans." (for "translated by") and the name of the translator.

Tolstoy, Leo. Anna Karenina. Trans. Constance

  Garnett. Indianapolis: Bobbs, 1978.

CORPORATE AUTHOR Begin with the name of the corporate author, even if it is also the name of the publisher.

Maryland Commission for Women. How to Translate

  Volunteer Skills into Employment Credentials.

  Baltimore: MD Commission for Women, 1979.

UNKNOWN AUTHOR Begin with the title. Alphabetize the entry by the first word of the title other than *a, an,* or *the.*

The Times Atlas of the World. 5th ed. New York:

  New York Times, 1975.

EDITION OTHER THAN THE FIRST If you are citing an edition other than the first, include the number of the edition after the title: 2nd ed., 3rd ed., and so on.

```
Spatt, Brenda.   Writing from Sources.   2nd ed.

     New York: St. Martin's, 1987.
```

MULTIVOLUME WORK   Include the number of volumes before the city and publisher, using the abbreviation "vols."

```
Graves, Robert.   The Greek Myths.   2 vols.   New York:

     Braziller, 1967.
```

If your paper cites only one of the volumes, write the volume number before the city and publisher and write the total number of volumes in the work after the date.

```
Graves, Robert.   The Greek Myths.   Vol. 2.   New York:

     Braziller, 1967. 2 vols.
```

WORK IN AN ANTHOLOGY   Present the information in this order, with each item followed by a period: author of the work; title of the work; title of the anthology; editor or editors of the anthology, preceded by "Ed."; city, publisher, and date; page numbers on which the work appears.

```
Abrams, M. H.   "English Romanticism: The Spirit of the

     Age."   Romanticism Reconsidered.   Ed. Northrop

     Frye.   New York: Columbia UP, 1963.   63-88.
```

ENCYCLOPEDIA OR DICTIONARY   Articles in well-known dictionaries and encyclopedias are handled in abbreviated form. Simply list the author of the article (if there is one), the title of the article, the title of the reference work, and the date of the edition.

```
Frankel, Mark S.   "Human Experimentation: Social

     and Professional Control."   Encyclopedia of

     Bioethics.   1978 ed.
```

Volume and page numbers are not necessary because the entries are arranged alphabetically and therefore are easy to locate.

If a reference work is not well known, include the city and the publisher as well.

GOVERNMENT PUBLICATION   Treat the government agency as the author, giving the name of the government followed by the name of the agency.

```
United States.   Internal Revenue Service.   Tax Guide
```

> for Small Business. Publication 334.
>
> Washington: GPO, 1983.

ARTICLE IN A MONTHLY MAGAZINE   In addition to the author, the title of the article, and the title of the magazine, list the month and year and the page numbers on which the article may be found. Abbreviate the names of months except May, June, and July.

> Lorenz, Wanda L. "Problem Areas in Accounting for
>
> Income Taxes." The Practical Accountant Feb.
>
> 1984: 69-77.

If the article appeared on pages 69–71 and 89–95, you would write "69 + " (not "69–95").

ARTICLE IN A WEEKLY MAGAZINE   Handle articles in weekly (or biweekly) magazines as you do those for monthly magazines, but give the exact date of the issue, not just the month and year.

> Clark, Matt. "Medicine: A Brave New World."
>
> Newsweek 5 Mar. 1984: 64-70.

ARTICLE IN A JOURNAL PAGINATED BY VOLUME   Many professional journals continue page numbers throughout the year instead of beginning each issue with page 1; at the end of the year, all of the issues are collected in a volume. Interested readers can find the article if they know only the volume number, the year, and the page numbers.

> Otto, Mary L. "Child Abuse: Group Treatment for
>
> Parents." Personnel and Guidance Journal 62
>
> (1984): 336-38.

ARTICLE IN A JOURNAL PAGINATED BY ISSUE   If each issue of the journal begins with page 1, you need to indicate the number of the issue. Simply place a period and the number of the issue after the volume number.

> Nichols, Randall G. "Word Processing and Basic
>
> Writers." Journal of Basic Writing 5.2 (1986):
>
> 81-97.

ARTICLE IN A DAILY NEWSPAPER   Begin with the author, if there is one, followed by the title of the article. Next list the name of the newspaper, the date, the section letter or number, and the page number.

> Gorney, Cynthia. "When the Gorilla Speaks."
>
> Washington Post 31 Jan. 1985: B1.

If the section is marked with a number rather than a letter, handle the entry as follows.

> "Market Leaks: Illegal Insider Trading Seems to Be
>
> on Rise: Ethical Issues Muddled." Wall Street
>
> Journal 2 Mar. 1984, sec. 1: 1.

If an edition of the newspaper is specified on the masthead, name the edition after the date and before the page reference: eastern ed., late ed., natl. ed., and so on.

FILMS AND TELEVISION PROGRAMS Begin with the title and the director and end with the distributor and the year. After the name of the director, include other information if you wish, such as the names of lead actors.

> North by Northwest. Dir. Alfred Hitchcock. With
>
> Cary Grant. MGM, 1959.

LIVE PERFORMANCE OF A PLAY Begin with the title of the play, followed by the author. Then include specific information about the live performance: the director, the major actors, the theater company and its location, and the date of the performance.

> Mother Courage. By Bertolt Brecht. Dir. Timothy
>
> Mayer. With Linda Hunt. Boston Shakespeare
>
> Company Theater, Boston. 20 Jan. 1984.

RECORDING Begin with the composer (or author, if the recording is spoken), followed by the title of the piece. Next list the pertinent artists (for instance, the conductor, the pianist, or the reader). End with the company label, the catalog number, and the date.

> Handel, George Frederick. Messiah. With Elizabeth
>
> Harwood, Janet Baker, Paul Esswood, Robert Tear,
>
> and Raimund Herincz. Cond. Charles Mackerras.
>
> English Chamber Orch. and the Ambrosian Singers.
>
> Angel, R 67-2682, 1967.

COMPUTER SOFTWARE   Begin with the author of the program (if known), the title of the program, and the words "Computer software," each followed by a period. Then name the distributor and the year of publication. At the end of the entry you may add other pertinent information, such as the computer for which the program is designed or the form of the program.

> Childpace. Computer software. Computerose, 1984.
>
>> Commodore 64, disk.

INTERVIEW   Begin with the name of the person interviewed. Next write "Personal interview." End with the date of the interview.

> Shaw, Lloyd. Personal interview. 21 Mar. 1987.

TWO OR MORE WORKS BY THE SAME AUTHOR   If your list of works cited includes two or more works by the same author, use the author's name only for the first entry. For subsequent entries use three hyphens followed by a period. List the titles in alphabetical order.

> Davis, Flora. Eloquent Animals: A Study in Animal
>
>> Communication. New York: Coward, 1978.
>
> ---. Inside Intuition: What We Know About Nonverbal
>
>> Communication. New York: McGraw, 1973.

D4

APA style

The American Psychological Association (APA) recommends in-text citations that refer the reader to a list of references (works cited).

D4-a APA in-text citations

The APA's in-text citations provide at least the author's last name and the date of publication. For direct quotations, a page number is given as well.

BASIC FORMAT FOR A QUOTATION   Ordinarily, introduce the quotation with a signal phrase that includes the author's last name followed by the date of publication in parentheses. Put the page number in parentheses at the end of the quotation.

> As Davis (1978) reports, "If the existence of a sign-
> ing ape was unsettling for linguists, it was also
> startling news for animal behaviorists" (p. 26).

When the author's name does not appear in the signal phrase, place the author's name, the date, and the page number in parentheses at the end. Use commas between items in the parentheses.

BASIC FORMAT FOR A SUMMARY OR A PARAPHRASE For a summary or a paraphrase, include the author's last name and the date either in a signal phrase or in parentheses at the end. A page number is not required.

> According to Davis (1978), when they learned of an
> ape's ability to use sign language, both linguists and
> animal behaviorists were taken by surprise.

> When they learned of an ape's ability to use sign
> language, both linguists and animal behaviorists were
> taken by surprise (Davis, 1978).

A WORK WITH TWO OR MORE AUTHORS If your source has two authors, name both in the signal phrase or parentheses each time cited; in the parentheses, use "&" (not "and").

> Patterson and Linden (1981) agree that the gorilla
> Koko acquired language more slowly than a normal
> speaking child.

If your source has three, four, or five authors, identify all of them the first time you cite the source.

> The team of researchers also warned that the fishing
> industry on the Chesapeake Bay is threatened by pol-
> lution (Blake, Simon, & McCann, 1987).

In subsequent citations, use only the first author's name followed by "et al." in the signal phrase or parentheses.

> The team of researchers also warned that the fishing

industry on the Chesapeake Bay is threatened by pol-

lution (Blake et al., 1987).

If your source has six or more authors, use only the first author's name followed by "et al." in all citations.

AUTHOR UNKNOWN If the author is not given, either use the complete title in a signal phrase or use the first two or three words of the title in the parenthetical citation.

The UFO reported by the crew of a Japan Air Lines

flight remains a mystery. Radar tapes did not con-

firm the presence of another craft ("Strange Encoun-

ter," 1987).

If "Anonymous" is specified as the author, treat it as if it were a real name: (Anonymous, 1987). In the list of references, also use the name Anonymous as author.

CORPORATE AUTHOR If the author is a government agency or other corporate organization with a long and cumbersome name, spell out the name the first time you use it in a citation, followed by an abbreviation in brackets. In later citations, simply use the abbreviation.

First citation: (National Institute of Mental Health
                   [NIMH], 1981)

Later citations: (NIMH, 1981)

TWO OR MORE WORKS IN THE SAME PARENTHESES When your parenthetical citation names two or more works, put them in the same order that they appear in the list of references, separated by semicolons.

AUTHORS WITH THE SAME LAST NAME To avoid confusion, use initials with the last names if your list of references contains two or more authors with the same last name.

Research by J. A. Smith (1987) revealed that. . . .

PERSONAL COMMUNICATION Conversations, memos, letters, and similar unpublished person-to-person communications should be cited by initials, last name, and precise date.

```
L. Smith (personal communication, October 12, 1987)
predicts that government funding of this type of re-
search will end soon.
```

Do not include personal communications in the list of references at the end of your paper.

D4-b APA references (list of works cited)

In APA style, the alphabetical list of works cited is entitled "References." The general principles are as follows:

1. Invert *all* authors' names and use initials instead of first names. With two or more authors, use an ampersand (&) rather than the word "and."
2. Use all authors' names; do not use "et al."
3. Place the date in parentheses immediately after the last author's name.
4. Underline titles and subtitles of books: capitalize only the first word of the title and subtitle (as well as all proper nouns).
5. Do not place titles of articles in quotation marks, and capitalize only the first word of the title and subtitle (and all proper nouns). Capitalize names of periodicals as you would capitalize them ordinarily (see M1-c). Underline the volume number of periodicals.
6. Use the abbreviation "p." (or "pp." for plural) before page numbers of magazine and newspaper articles and works in anthologies, but do not use them before page numbers of articles appearing in scholarly journals.
7. You may use a short form of the publisher's name as long as it is easily identifiable.
8. Alphabetize your list by the last name of the author (or editor); if there is no author or editor, alphabetize by the first word of the title other than *a, an,* or *the.*
9. Do not indent the first line of an entry but indent any additional lines.

BASIC FORMAT FOR A BOOK

```
Linden, E. (1986).  Silent partners: The legacy of
    the ape language experiments.  New York: Random
    House.
```

TWO OR MORE AUTHORS

Patterson, F., & Linden, E. (1981). <u>The education of</u>
<u>Koko</u>. New York: Holt, Rinehart and Winston.

EDITORS

Sebeok, T. A., & Umiker-Sebeok, J. (Eds.). (1980).
<u>Speaking of apes</u>. New York: Plenum Press.

EDITION OTHER THAN THE FIRST

Falk, J. S. (1978). <u>Linguistics and language: A</u>
<u>survey of basic concepts and implications</u>
(2nd ed.). New York: Wiley.

WORK IN AN ANTHOLOGY

Basso, K. H. Silence in western Apache culture.
(1970). In P. Giglioli (Ed.), <u>Language and</u>
<u>social context</u> (pp. 67-86). Harmondsworth,
England: Penguin.

ARTICLE IN A JOURNAL PAGINATED BY VOLUME

Otto, M. L. (1984). Child abuse: Group treatment for
parents. <u>Personnel and Guidance Journal</u>, <u>62</u>,
336-338.

ARTICLE IN A JOURNAL PAGINATED BY ISSUE

Nichols, R. G. (1986). Word processing and basic
writers. <u>Journal of Basic Writing</u>, <u>5</u>(2), 81-97.

ARTICLE IN A MAGAZINE

Seyfarth, R. M. (1982, March-April). Talking with
monkeys and great apes. <u>International Wildlife</u>,
pp. 13-18.

TWO OR MORE WORKS BY THE SAME AUTHOR Use the author's
name for first and subsequent entries. Arrange the entries by date,
the earliest first.

Davis, F. (1973). <u>Inside intuition: What we know
about nonverbal communication</u>. New York:
McGraw-Hill.

Davis, F. (1978). <u>Eloquent animals: A study in
animal communication</u>. New York: Coward,
McCann & Geoghegan.

D5

Footnotes or endnotes

Until 1984 the Modern Language Association's *MLA Handbook* recommended footnotes or endnotes instead of in-text citations. Although the current (1988) *MLA Handbook* treats in-text citations as its preferred style (see D3-a), it also lists the traditional notes as an acceptable alternative.

Notes provide complete publishing information, either at the bottom of the page (footnotes) or at the end of the paper (endnotes). A raised arabic numeral in the text indicates that a quotation, paraphrase, or summary has been borrowed from a source; to find the publishing information for that source, readers consult the footnote or endnote with the corresponding number. Notes are numbered consecutively throughout the paper.

TEXT

For instance, Lana once described a cucumber as
"banana which-is green."[9]

NOTE

[9] Flora Davis, <u>Eloquent Animals: A Study in
Animal Communication</u> (New York: Coward, 1978) 300.

The first time you cite a source in your paper, the note should include the full publication information for that work as well as the page number of the specific quotation, paraphrase, or summary. The following examples cover the formats that are most frequently encountered.

BASIC FORMAT FOR A BOOK

   [1] Eugene Linden, <u>Silent Partners: The Legacy of</u>
<u>the Ape Language Experiments</u> (New York: Random, 1986)
87.

TWO OR MORE AUTHORS

   [2] Roger Fisher and William Ury, <u>Getting to Yes</u>:
<u>Negotiating Agreement without Giving In</u> (Boston:
Houghton, 1981) 108.

EDITOR OR TRANSLATOR

   [3] Albert Camus, <u>Lyrical and Critical Essays</u>,
trans. Ellen Conroy Kennedy, ed. Philip Thody
(New York: Knopf, 1968) 8.

UNKNOWN AUTHOR

   [4] <u>The Times Atlas of the World</u>, 5th ed.
(New York: New York Times, 1975) 95.

EDITION OTHER THAN THE FIRST

   [5] Brenda Spatt, <u>Writing from Sources</u>, 2nd ed.
(New York: St Martin's, 1987) 78.

MULTIVOLUME WORK

   [6] Robert Graves, <u>The Greek Myths</u>, vol. 2 (New
York: Braziller, 1967) 216.

WORK IN AN ANTHOLOGY

   [7] M. H. Abrams, "English Romanticism: The Spirit
of the Age," <u>Romanticism Reconsidered</u>, ed. Northrop
Frye (New York: Columbia UP, 1963) 64.

ENCYCLOPEDIA OR DICTIONARY

   [8] Mark S. Frankel, "Human Experimentation: Social
and Professional Control," <u>Encyclopedia of Bioethics</u>,
1978 ed.

ARTICLE IN A MAGAZINE

9 Matt Clark, "Medicine: A Brave New World," <u>Newsweek</u> 5 Mar. 1984: 65.

ARTICLE IN A JOURNAL PAGINATED BY VOLUME

10 Mary L. Otto, "Child Abuse: Group Treatment for Parents," <u>Personnel and Guidance Journal</u> 62 (1984): 336.

ARTICLE IN A JOURNAL PAGINATED BY ISSUE

11 Randall G. Nichols, "Word Processing and Basic Writers," <u>Journal of Basic Writing</u> 5.2 (1986): 93.

ARTICLE IN A NEWSPAPER

12 Cynthia Gorney, "When the Gorilla Speaks," <u>Washington Post</u> 31 Jan. 1985: B1.

SUBSEQUENT REFERENCES TO THE SAME SOURCE   Subsequent references to a work that has already been cited in a note should be given in shortened form. You need to give only enough information so that the reader can identify which work you are referring to — usually the author's last name and a page number. The abbreviations *ibid.* and *op. cit.* are no longer used.

13 Linden 129.

14 Fisher and Ury 16.

If you are using more than one work by one author or two works by authors with the same last name, cite the author's last name and a shortened title.

15 Linden. <u>Silent</u> 53.

16 Linden. <u>Apes</u> 136.

When you use notes as your method of documentation, you may not need a list of works cited, since complete publishing information is given in the notes themselves. Some professors prefer, however, that you include an alphabetized list of the works cited in the paper or a bibliography of the works you consulted, whether or not they were cited. If you do include a list of works cited or a bibliography, use the MLA style described in D3-b.

Review of
Basic Grammar

Index

R

Review of Basic Grammar

R1

Parts of speech

The parts of speech are a system for classifying words. There are eight parts of speech: noun, pronoun, verb, adjective, adverb, preposition, conjunction, and interjection. Many words can function as more than one part of speech. For example, depending on its use in a sentence, the word *paint* can be a noun (*The paint is wet*) or a verb (*Please paint the ceiling next*).

R1-a Nouns

A noun is the name of a person, place, thing, or idea. Nouns are often but not always signaled by an article (*a, an, the*).

> The *cat* in *gloves* catches no *mice*.
>
> *Repetition* does not transform a *lie* into *truth*.

Nouns sometimes function as adjectives modifying other nouns.

> You can't make a *silk* purse out of a *sow's* ear.

Nouns are classified for a variety of purposes. When capitalization is the issue, we speak of *proper* versus *common* nouns (see M1-a). If the problem is one of word choice, we may speak of *concrete* versus *abstract* nouns (see W4-b). Most nouns come in *singular* and *plural* forms; *collective* nouns may be either singular or plural (see G1-e and G3-a). *Possessive* nouns require an apostrophe (see P5-a).

R1-b Pronouns

A pronoun is a word used in place of a noun. Usually the pronoun substitutes for a specific noun, known as its *antecedent*.

> When the *wheel* squeaks, *it* is greased.

Most of the pronouns in English are listed in this section.

PERSONAL PRONOUNS Personal pronouns refer to specific persons or things.

Singular: I, me, you, she, her, he, him, it

Plural: we, us, you, they, them

POSSESSIVE PRONOUNS   Possessive pronouns indicate ownership.

Singular: my, mine, your, yours, her, hers, his, its

Plural: our, ours, your, yours, their, theirs

INTENSIVE AND REFLEXIVE PRONOUNS   Intensive pronouns emphasize a noun or another pronoun (The congresswoman *herself* met us at the door). Reflexive pronouns name a receiver of an action identical with the doer of the action (Paula cut *herself*).

Singular: myself, yourself, himself, herself, itself

Plural: ourselves, yourselves, themselves

RELATIVE PRONOUNS   Relative pronouns introduce adjective clauses (see R3-e).

who, whoever, whom, whomever, whose, which, that

INTERROGATIVE PRONOUNS   Interrogative pronouns introduce questions.

who, whom, whose, which, what

DEMONSTRATIVE PRONOUNS   Demonstrative pronouns point to nouns.

this, that, these, those

INDEFINITE PRONOUNS   Indefinite pronouns refer to nonspecific persons or things.

all, another, any, anybody, anyone, anything, both, each, either, everybody, everyone, everything, few, many, neither, nobody, none, no one, nothing, one, several, some, somebody, someone, something

R1-c Verbs

The verb of a sentence usually expresses action (*jump, think*) or being (*is, become*). It is composed of a main verb (MV) possibly preceded by one or more helping verbs (HV).

MV
The best fish *swim* near the bottom.

HV   MV
A marriage *is* not *built* in a day.

There are twenty-three helping verbs in English. Nine of them, called *modals,* function only as helping verbs, never as main verbs:

can, will, shall, should, could, would, may, might, must

The others may function either as helping verbs or as main verbs:

have, has, had
do, does, did
be, am, is, are, was, were, being, been

The main verb of a sentence is always the kind of word that would change form if put into these test sentences:

INFINITIVE FORM	Today I (*walk, ride*).
-S FORM	Today he/she/it (*walks, rides*).
PAST TENSE	Yesterday I (*walked, rode*).
PAST PARTICIPLE	I have (*walked, ridden*) many times before.
PRESENT PARTICIPLE	I am (*walking, riding*) right now.

When both the past-tense and the past-participle forms of a verb end in *-ed,* the verb is regular (*walked, walked*). Otherwise, the verb is irregular (*rode, ridden*). (See G2-a.)

The verb *be* is highly irregular, having eight forms instead of the usual five: the infinitive *be,* the present-tense forms *am, is,* and *are,* the past-tense forms *was* and *were,* the present participle *being,* and the past participle *been.*

Helping verbs combine with the various forms of main verbs to create tenses. For a chart of the major tenses, see G2-c.

R1-d Adjectives and articles

An adjective is a word used to modify, or describe, a noun or pronoun. An adjective usually answers one of these questions: Which one? What kind of? How many?

A *wild* goose never laid a *tame* egg.

If triangles had a god, it would have *three* sides.

Adjectives usually precede the words they modify. However, they may also follow linking verbs, in which case they describe the subject. (See R2-b.)

Good medicine always tastes *bitter*.

Articles, sometimes classified as adjectives, are used to mark nouns. There are only three: the definite article *the* and the indefinite articles *a* and *an*.

A country can be judged by *the* quality of its proverbs.

For use of *a* and *an,* see W1.

R1-e Adverbs

An adverb is a word used to modify a verb (or verbal), an adjective, or another adverb. It usually answers one of these questions: When? Where? How? Why? Under what conditions? To what degree?

Pull *gently* at a weak rope. [Pull how?]

Read the best books *first*. [Read when?]

Adverbs modifying adjectives or other adverbs usually intensify or limit the intensity of the word they modify.

Be *extremely* good, and you will be *very* lonesome.

The negators *not* and *never* are classified as adverbs.

R1-f Prepositions

A preposition is a word placed before a noun or pronoun to form a phrase modifying another word in the sentence. The prepositional phrase nearly always functions as an adjective or as an adverb.

The road *to hell* is paved *with good intentions*.

To hell functions as an adjective modifying the noun *road; with good intentions* functions as an adverb, modifying the verb *is paved*.

There are a limited number of prepositions in English. The most common are included in the following list.

about	beside	from	outside	toward
above	besides	in	over	under
across	between	inside	past	underneath
after	beyond	into	plus	unlike
against	but	like	regarding	until
along	by	near	respecting	unto
among	concerning	next	round	up
around	considering	of	since	upon
as	despite	off	than	with
at	down	on	through	without
before	during	onto	throughout	
behind	except	opposite	till	
below	for	out	to	

Some prepositions are more than one word long. *Along with, as well as, in addition to, next to,* and *up to* are common examples.

R1-g Conjunctions

Conjunctions join words, phrases, or clauses, and they indicate the relation between the elements joined.

COORDINATING CONJUNCTIONS Coordinating conjunctions connect grammatically equal elements.

and, but, or, nor, for, so, yet

CORRELATIVE CONJUNCTIONS Correlative conjunctions are pairs of conjunctions that connect grammatically equal elements.

either . . . or, neither . . . nor, not only . . . but also, whether . . . or, both . . . and

SUBORDINATING CONJUNCTIONS Subordinating conjunctions introduce subordinate clauses and indicate their relation to the rest of the sentence. (See R3-e.)

after, although, as, as if, because, before, even though, if, in order that, rather than, since, so that, than, that, though, unless, until, when, where, whether, while

NOTE: The following relative pronouns also introduce subordinate clauses: *who, whom, whoever, whomever, whose, which,* and *that.*

CONJUNCTIVE ADVERBS Conjunctive adverbs are adverbs used to indicate the relation between independent clauses. (See G6-b and P3-a.)

> finally, furthermore, however, moreover, nevertheless, similarly, then, therefore, thus

R1-h Interjections

Interjections are words used to express surprise or emotion (*Oh! Hey! Wow!*).

R2

Parts of sentences

Most English sentences flow from subject to verb to any objects or complements. *Predicate* is the grammatical term given to the verb plus its objects, complements, and modifiers.

R2-a Subjects

The subject of a sentence names who or what the sentence is about. The simple subject is always a noun or a pronoun; the complete subject consists of the simple subject and all of its modifiers.

COMPLETE SUBJECT
SS
The purity of a revolution usually lasts about two weeks.

COMPLETE
SUBJECT
SS
In every country, *the sun* rises in the morning.

A sentence may have a compound subject containing two or more simple subjects joined with a coordinating conjunction such as, *and* or *or.*

SS   SS
Much industry and little conscience make us rich.

In imperative sentences, which give advice or commands, the subject is an understood *you.*

[You] Hitch your wagon to a star.

Although the subject ordinarily comes before the verb, occasionally it does not. When a sentence begins with *there is* or *there are* (or *there was* or *there were*), the subject follows the verb. The word *there* is an expletive in such constructions, an empty word serving merely to get the sentence started.

SS
There is *no substitute for victory.*

Sometimes a writer will invert a sentence for effect.

SS
Happy is *the nation that has no history.*

In questions, the subject frequently appears in an unusual position, sandwiched between parts of the verb.

SS
Do *married men* make the best husbands?

R2-b Verbs, objects, and complements

Section R1-c explains how to identify verbs. A sentence's verb(s) may be classified as linking, transitive, or intransitive, depending on the kinds of objects or complements the verb can (or cannot) take.

Linking verbs and subject complements

Linking verbs (V) take subject complements (SC), words or word groups that complete the meaning of the subject (S) by either renaming it or describing it.

⎡————S————⎤ V ⎡————SC————⎤
The quarrels of friends are the opportunities of foes.

⎡S⎤ V ⎡SC⎤
Love is blind.

When the simple subject complement renames the subject, it is a noun or pronoun, such as *opportunities;* when it describes the subject, it is an adjective, such as *blind.*

Linking verbs are usually a form of *be: be, am, is, are, was, were, being, been.* Verbs such as *appear, become, feel, grow, look, make, prove, seem, smell, sound,* and *taste* are linking when they are followed by a word group that names or describes the subject.

Transitive verbs and direct objects

Transitive verbs take direct objects (DO), words or word groups that complete the meaning of the verb by naming the receiver of the action. The simple direct object is always a noun or a pronoun.

$$\overline{S}\quad V\quad \overline{DO}$$
The little snake studies the ways of the big serpent.

Transitive verbs usually appear in the active voice, with the subject doing the action and a direct object receiving the action. Active-voice sentences can be transformed into the passive voice, with the subject receiving the action instead.

ACTIVE VOICE   The early bird catches the worm.

PASSIVE VOICE   The early worm is sometimes caught by the early bird.

What was once the direct object (*the worm*) has become the subject in the passive-voice transformation, and the original subject appears in a prepositional phrase beginning with *by.* The *by* phrase is frequently omitted in passive-voice constructions: *The early worm is sometimes caught.*

Transitive verbs, indirect objects, and direct objects

The direct object of a transitive verb is sometimes preceded by an indirect object (IO), a noun or pronoun telling to whom or for whom the action of the sentence is done.

You show [to] me a hero, and I will write [for] you a tragedy.

Transitive verbs, direct objects, and object complements

The direct object of a transitive verb is sometimes followed by an object complement (OC), a word or word group that completes the direct object's meaning by renaming or describing it.

<pre>
   ┌────S────┐ V ┌─DO─┐┌───────────OC───────────┐
</pre>
Some people call a spade an agricultural implement.

<pre>
   ┌─S─┐ V   ┌─────DO─────┐┌─OC─┐
</pre>
Love makes all hard hearts gentle.

When the object complement renames the direct object, it is a noun or pronoun, such as *implement*. When it describes the direct object, it is an adjective, such as *gentle*.

Intransitive verbs

Intransitive verbs take no objects or complements. They may or may not be followed by adverbial modifiers.

<pre>
      S   V
</pre>
Money talks.

<pre>
      S   V
</pre>
All roads lead to Rome.

R3

Subordinate word groups

Subordinate word groups cannot stand alone. They function within sentences usually as adjectives, adverbs, or nouns.

R3-a Prepositional phrases

A prepositional phrase begins with a preposition such as *at, by, for, from, in, of, on, to,* or *with* (see R1-f) and ends with a noun or a noun equivalent. The noun or noun equivalent is known as the object of the preposition.

Prepositional phrases nearly always function as adjectives or as adverbs. When functioning as an adjective, a prepositional phrase appears immediately following the noun or pronoun it modifies.

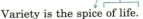
Variety is the spice of life.

When functioning as an adverb, a prepositional phrase may or may not appear next to the verb it modifies.

Do not judge a tree by its bark.

R3-b Verbal phrases

A verbal is a verb form that does not function as the verb of a clause. Verbals include infinitives (the word *to* plus the dictionary form of the verb), present participles (the *-ing* form of the verb), and past participles (the form of the verb that can follow *have*, often ending in *-ed* or *-en*) (see R1-c).

Verbals can take objects, complements, and modifiers to form verbal phrases. These phrases are classified as participial, gerund, and infinitive.

Participial phrases

Participial phrases always function as adjectives. Their verbals are either present participles or past participles.

Being a philosopher, I have a problem for every solution.

Truth *kept in the dark* will never save the world.

Gerund phrases

Gerund phrases always function as nouns: usually as subjects, subject complements, direct objects, or objects of the preposition. Their verbals are present participles.

Justifying a fault doubles it.

Kleptomaniacs can't help *helping themselves.*

Infinitive phrases

Infinitive phrases function as adjectives, adverbs, or nouns. Their verbals are always infinitives.

We do not have the right *to abandon the poor*.

He cut off his nose *to spite his face*.

To side with truth is noble.

R3-c Appositive phrases

Appositive phrases describe nouns or pronouns. In form they are nouns or noun equivalents.

> Politicians, *acrobats at heart,* can sit on a fence and yet keep both ears to the ground.

R3-d Absolute phrases

An absolute phrase modifies a whole clause or sentence, not just one word. It consists of a noun or noun equivalent usually followed by a participial phrase.

> *His words dipped in honey,* the senator mesmerized the crowd.

R3-e Subordinate clauses

Subordinate clauses are patterned like sentences, having subjects and verbs and sometimes objects or complements, but they function within sentences as adjectives, adverbs, or nouns. They cannot stand alone as complete sentences.

Adjective clauses

Adjective clauses modify nouns or pronouns, usually answering one of these questions: Which one? What kind of? They begin with a relative pronoun (*who, whoever, whom, whomever, whose, which,* or *that*) or a relative adverb (*when* or *where*).

The arrow *that has left the bow* never returns.

Adverb clauses

Adverb clauses modify verbs, adjectives, or other adverbs, usually answering one of these questions: When? Where? Why? How? Under what conditions? To what degree? They begin with a subordinating conjunction (*after, although, as, as if, because, before, even though, if, in order that, rather than, since, so that, than, that, though, unless, until, when, where, whether, while*).

When the well is dry, we know the worth of water.

Venice would be a fine city if it were only drained.

Noun clauses

Noun clauses function as subjects, objects, or complements. They usually begin with one of the following subordinating conjunctions: *that, who, whoever, whom, whomever, what, whatever, how, when, where, whether.*

Whoever gossips to you will gossip of you.

R4

Sentence types

Depending on the number and type of clauses they contain, sentences are classified as simple, compound, complex, or compound-complex.

Clauses come in two varieties: independent and subordinate. An independent clause contains a subject and predicate, and it either stands alone or could stand alone. A subordinate clause also contains a subject and predicate, but it functions within a sentence as an adjective, an adverb, or a noun; it cannot stand alone.

SIMPLE SENTENCE   A simple sentence is one independent clause with no subordinate clauses.

┌─────────INDEPENDENT CLAUSE─────────┐
Without music, life would be a mistake.

COMPOUND SENTENCE   A compound sentence is composed of two or more independent clauses with no subordinate clauses. The independent clauses are usually joined with a comma and a coordinating conjunction (*and, but, or, nor, for, so, yet*) or with a semicolon.

┌─INDEPENDENT CLAUSE─┐   ┌─INDEPENDENT CLAUSE─┐
One arrow is easily broken, but you can't break a bundle of ten.

COMPLEX SENTENCE   A complex sentence is composed of one independent clause with one or more subordinate clauses.

┌─SUBORDINATE─┐
│   CLAUSE   │
If you scatter thorns, don't go barefoot.

COMPOUND-COMPLEX SENTENCE   A compound-complex sentence contains at least two independent clauses and at least one subordinate clause. The following sentence contains two independent clauses, each of which contains a subordinate clause.

┌────IND CLAUSE────┐   ┌────IND CLAUSE────┐
  ┌─SUB CLAUSE─┐   ┌─SUB CLAUSE─┐
Tell me what you eat, and I will tell you what you are.

Index

Correction Symbols
Boldface numbers refer to sections of this book.

abbr	faulty abbreviation **M2**	**p**	error in punctuation	
ad	misuse of adverb or adjective **G4**	**⌄**	comma **P1**	
		no ,	no comma **P2**	
agr	faulty agreement **G1, G3-a**	**;**	semicolon **P3**	
appr	inappropriate language **W3**	**:**	colon **P4**	
		⌄'	apostrophe **P5**	
awk	awkward	**" "**	quotation marks **P6**	
cap	capital letter **M1**	**. ? !**	period, question mark, exclamation point **P7**	
case	error in case **G3-c, d**			
coh	coherence **C2-b**	**— ( ) [ ] . . . /**	dash, parentheses, brackets, ellipsis, slash **P8**	
coord	faulty coordination **E6-b**			
cs	comma splice **G6**	**par, ¶**	new paragraph **C2-b**	
dev	inadequate development **C2-b**	**pass**	ineffective passive **G2-e**	
		ref	error in pronoun reference **G3-b**	
dm	dangling modifier **E3-c**			
exact	inexact language **W4**	**shift**	distracting shift **E4**	
frag	sentence fragment **G5**	**sp**	misspelled word **M5**	
fs	fused sentence **G6**	**sub**	subordination needed **E6-d**	
hyph	error in use of hyphen **M6**	**sxt**	sexist language **W3-e**	
inc	incomplete construction **E2**	**t**	error in verb tense **G2-c**	
		trans	transition needed **C2-b**	
irreg	error in irregular verb **G2-a**	**us**	see glossary of usage **W1**	
ital	italics (underlining) **M4**	**var**	lack of variety in sentence structure **E7**	
jar	jargon **W3-a**			
lc	use lowercase letter **M1**	**vb**	error in verb form **G2**	
mixed	mixed construction **E5**	**w**	wordy **W2**	
mm	misplaced modifier **E3-b**	**wc**	word choice **W3, W4**	
mood	error in mood **G2-d**	**//**	faulty parallelism **E1**	
ms	manuscript form **M7**	**∧**	insert	
nonst	nonstandard usage **W3-c**	**x**	obvious error	
num	error in use of numbers **M3**	**#**	insert space	
om	omitted word **E2**	**⌣**	close up space	

Contents